THE SOCIAL WORK STUDENT'S RESEARCH HANDBOOK

This second edition of *The Social Work Student's Research Handbook* provides an essential guide for social work students beginning to participate in research. Practical and easy to use, this comprehensive handbook provides instant access to the nuts and bolts of social work research. Each chapter in this second edition has been updated to reflect the dynamic and changing nature of social work research, and three new topical chapters have been included that offer new food for thought on research context and ethics and on the role of evidence in professional practice.

The book is intended as a resource to complement the dense and heavy research books available. This text provides the tools that students need to fully engage with their research and is an essential reference aid for use alongside professional literature for selecting a problem for social work study with consideration of context and ethics; identifying a design type; developing or selecting an instrument; developing a sampling strategy; collecting and analyzing data; and organizing, writing, disseminating, and utilizing results in a politically sensitive way.

The Social Work Student's Research Handbook is an invaluable resource for undergraduate and graduate social work students as well as practitioners new to the field as they apply what they've learned in research courses toward consuming research effectively, implementing original research projects, and ultimately, becoming an evidence-based practitioner.

Dominique Moyse Steinberg is former Chair of the Social Group Work Sequence at Hunter College School of Social Work, USA, where she taught Social Group Work Practice for Group Work Majors, a Practice Lab, Research Methods, (Basic, Advanced, and Program and Practice Evaluation) and an Integrative Writing Seminar. On the adjunct faculty as of 1986, Steinberg left HCSSW in 1997 to teach at Smith College SSW until 2004, when she returned to HCSSW full time, assuming Chair of the sequence in 2005. A prolific writer with regular contributions to the professional literature, Steinberg has special interest in social work methods, mutual aid, practice ethics and effectiveness, elder care, conflict resolution, and communication. On the Editorial Boards of *Social Work with Groups* and *The Journal of Teaching in Social Work*, in addition to being a member of IASWG since 1985 and Treasurer of IASWG since 2007, Steinberg is also a member of NASW and ACR, and an ACSW Fellow. She currently teaches graduate research courses for Simmons College SSW online, advises thesis projects for Smith College SSW, offers elder-care resources online (www.customeldercare.org), and is Director of Group Work Services for The Project for Team Conferencing and Social Group Work, Inc., a non-profit training agency in New York City (http://theteamconferenceandgroupworkproject.org).

THE SOCIAL WORK STUDENT'S RESEARCH HANDBOOK

Second edition

Dominique Moyse Steinberg

LONDON AND NEW YORK

First published 2004
by The Haworth Social Work Practice Press, an imprint of The Haworth Press, Inc.
Alice Street, Binghamton, NY 13904-1580.

This edition published 2015
by Routledge
2 Park Square, Milton Park, Abingdon, Oxon OX14 4RN
and by Routledge
711 Third Avenue, New York, NY 10017

Routledge is an imprint of the Taylor & Francis Group, an informa business

British Library Cataloguing-in-Publication Data
A catalogue record for this book is available from the British Library

Library of Congress Cataloging in Publication Data
Steinberg, Dominique Moyse, author.
The social work student's research handbook / written by Dominique Moyse Steinberg. -- Second edition.
pages cm
Includes bibliographical references and index.
1. Social service--Research--Handbooks, manuals, etc. 2. Social service--Research--Methodology. 3. Social work education. I. Title.
[DNLM: 1. Social Work--education. 2. Research Design. HV 11]
HV11.S77 2015
361.3072--dc23
2014049452

ISBN: 978-1-138-84409-4 (hbk)
ISBN: 978-1-138-91082-9 (pbk)
ISBN: 978-1-315-73062-2 (ebk)

Typeset in Bembo
by Saxon Graphics Ltd, Derby

Printed and bound in the United States of America by Publishers Graphics, LLC on sustainably sourced paper.

I dedicate this book to my late husband, Irwin Steinberg, with gratitude for forty years of lionhearted support.

CONTENTS

PREFACE

Ten years after writing the first edition of this handbook, social work research courses continue to be required by the Council on Social Work Education; engaging in scientific inquiry is ever more specifically required by the National Association of Social Workers *Code of Ethics*; from all corners of the globe come calls for "evidence-based" practice, and the literature abounds with articles and books about the nature, role, and meaning of evidence in social work. Ten years ago, I said, *that's a lot of attention on research!* Today, I say, *attention to the place of research is even more widespread*, while years of continuing professional practice, teaching, and conversations with colleagues continue to suggest that most people who enter social work still do not describe themselves as "scientifically minded" and still come to the field frightened, even phobic, of research. In fact, it continues to be commonplace to hear social work students say that they have chosen the field because of its humanistic, experiential, and interactive values rather than because of a focus on scientific inquiry.

I still hear many students and new practitioners say, *I didn't enter social work to engage in math or science ... I entered it to help people!* And over these last ten years since the first edition of this handbook, I continue to encounter a common thread of resistance to learning (and even thinking) about research—"research as a necessary evil of social work education." And of course, I continue to hope using this handbook will change many minds! From those who have used it, I have heard that it has in fact made learning research easier—that it has made the concepts and principles more accessible, and that as a result, students are less daunted about having to learn the subject and its role in practice. In fact, I received a letter not too long ago from a student who had been particularly resistant to the course content although she had done well. In this letter she proudly announced that she had been hired by an agency specifically to engage in research and thanked me for teaching her! What teacher could ask for more? I hope, therefore, that this handbook will help others like her to move from a position of, *Oh dear, I guess I have to learn this!* to one that has at the very least an understanding of (and maybe even appreciation for) inquiry as an essential tool of *professional* practice.

As a teacher I've also had opportunities to use various textbooks, including new editions over the last ten years. Most continue to be excellent, covering an enormous amount of material of which both intellectual and practical sense must be made. While it's appropriate for them to be comprehensive, however, as I said in the first edition, it is that very attempt to "cover it all" that has prompted this small and hopefully user-friendly handbook to help learners grasp the essential elements of good research, both as producers and consumers.

Clearly, integration of content should and is expected to occur through classroom process; but I hear complaints like the following ones over and over again. *The first chapter is okay, but then I get lost in all the technical stuff.* Or *The beginning on theory and philosophical underpinnings of research are so abstruse!* Or *I'm discouraged and even more anxious than before I started to read.* Or *I'm just so nervous about research that I'm afraid to even read about it!* In fact, I have even heard some students say that they find themselves underlining every sentence as they read because it is so difficult to extrapolate the supposedly essential material from surrounding discussion!

It is my hope, therefore, that this second edition will continue to be useful—that it will enhance the reader's ability to pick out the essential highlights of social research methods; that it will help the reader make better use of the classroom and better contribute to his/her own learning; that it will facilitate integration of research into other areas of professional work; and that ultimately, it will help the reader to become a better producer and consumer of social work research, and as such, a better social worker.

Dominique Moyse Steinberg
March 5, 2015

INTRODUCTION

The purpose of this handbook is to help you take and keep hold of the major concepts, principles, and steps of the research process using social work as context. There are many, many research books on the shelves today, most of them hundreds of pages and thousands of words in length. And many of them are very good. They speak to all of the issues from thinking about what to study (problem formulation) to why study it (professional significance) to different ways of inquiring (design and methodology) to how to talk about what you found (analysis and dissemination of results) usually including throughout those discussions special attention to ethics, both conceptually and methodologically. In other words, lots of material is covered in one place, and for many of us it can be difficult to pick out from all the narrative and details and examples those points that either must be kept in mind or need to be understood in order to move from one methodological step to the next.

This handbook, therefore, is intended to complement, not replace, those books. It's for reading after them or with them or even perhaps before them—for using in your own time as a refresher, say, after reading about problem formulation in order to help you cull the "nuts and bolts" of formulating your own problem for study. It is for reading while you are in the library or on the bus. It is for checking as someone speaks of correlational design or inferential stats and you find yourself saying, *Huh?* It's for using in the privacy and quiet of your thinking, outside of the classroom—for keeping the "operatic highlights" of the research process in mind as you move through what is admittedly both complex and simple (though not simplistic) at once.

Social work research books say pretty much the same thing. Authors have various points of view, of course, and their own personal ways of presenting the material, of trying to help you make sense of what they're saying. Some are more or less technical. Some are more or less verbose. Some are richer with better examples. Regardless of style, however, major points are always and unavoidably surrounded by thousands upon thousands of other words so that the highlights or major concepts and principles at the heart of the matter can easily get lost, subsumed by long theoretical narratives accompanied by example after example.

The purpose of this handbook, then, in a nutshell, is to help you wade through all that, to help you pick out what's really important—the "crux" of each issue. How so? First, it will help you feel better and more confident about engaging in research. For example, are there moments in formulating a research question when you think you should be getting clearer but you're getting more confused instead? As Chapter 4 says, that's okay. It happens to everyone. It's part and parcel of problem formulation; this handbook tells you that it's okay and normal and what to do next to become less overwhelmed, when and how to go with the flow. Second, it will help you clarify basic or central concepts and principles in each step of the method (by which is meant the research process, from "soup" to "nuts")—what you must consider at each decision-making point. Third, it will help you connect those steps to one another, both conceptually and practically. And fourth, it will help you integrate theory (what should be done) with the real world (what's feasible).

In addition, this second edition offers three more areas to explore. First, there is a brief overview of context. Context is everything to social work, with its systems and person-in-environment orientations. Chapter 1, therefore, tries to help you consider the context in which research is to take place, and issues to consider about the larger socio-political context, about the smaller context (such as your agency), and about your most personal context (your own preconceived notions, biases, professional ideology, etc.). Chapter 2 identifies the major concepts and issues related to research ethics in the context of professional social work practice, drawing on the National Association of Social Workers *Code of Ethics* (www. socialworkers.org/pubs/code/default.asp) to consider the guidelines for ethical research conduct. And third, Chapter 3 discusses the concept of evidence and its role in developing *informed* professional social work at all levels of service.

The next 22 chapters of this book are organized as follows: Chapter 4 describes and discusses problem formulation, the first and perhaps most challenging, artistic, but fun part of research, when you have an opportunity to play around with and decide which of all possible questions you'd like to ask. Chapter 5, devoted to reviewing the literature, will help you understand why and how to read and think about what others have said and done in your topic of interest, especially in the empirical literature. Chapter 6 describes the role of and discusses similarities and differences between hypotheses and research questions and the implications of working from either one. Chapter 7 talks about variables—how to conceptualize, define, and measure them. Chapter 8 explains the role (and potential danger) of assumptions. Chapter 9 on design options provides an overview of each of four research design types and clarifies the connection between a study's purpose and selecting design. Chapters 10 through 13 describe in greater detail exploratory, descriptive, experimental, and correlational design (also referred to as quasi-experimental design), respectively. Chapter 14 explains the role of plausible alternative (rival) explanations in experimental and correlational design types. Chapter 15 presents the major concepts and principles of practice evaluation, along with examples of a few basic designs. Chapter 16 presents an overview of program evaluation and a brief discussion of logic models, an increasingly common program evaluation tool. Chapter 17 describes the role and meaning of reliability and validity in instrument design. Chapter 18 outlines and discusses the methods and implications of various sampling strategies. Major advantages, disadvantages, and issues to consider of three major data collection methods are presented in Chapter 19. Chapter 20 offers an overview of data analysis. Chapter 21 outlines the major concepts, principles, and issues to consider in qualitative analysis. Both focusing on quantitative data analysis, Chapters 22 and 23 review the role and major concepts and principles of descriptive and inferential statistics, respectively. Chapter 24 offers an overview of a few common statistical tests. Finally, Chapter 25 wraps up the book with an endnote.

Examples are used as often as possible to illustrate major points. Each chapter ends with a list of major points to remember, and each chapter on methods (Chapters 4–24) offers at least one exercise intended to help you make some immediate and personal use of the chapter content.

1

SOCIAL WORK RESEARCH: CONTEXT AND POLITICS

Key concepts

assumptions
bias
competence
context
critical thinking
CSWE-EPAS
politics
research as practice
research in social work practice
scientific inquiry—ways of knowing
skepticism

Introduction

All science is political—from the largest context (changing trends in global interest) to the smallest (yourself—your values, world view, etc.). This means, in a nutshell, that all research is conducted within sets of *assumptions*—assumptions about what is, what should be, and why; assumptions that help to create a *context* for study. And once you accept this premise—that a myriad "little" ideas and judgments go into scientific inquiry (what's valuable to know and why)—then you must also accept the proposition that, ultimately, research is a political process. It may not be explicitly political in the sense of civics, but who gets funded for what and when is clearly and overtly political. In short, the areas of inquiry along with the kinds of related questions deemed to be of value at any given moment inherently reflect the geopolitical/socioeconomic values of the moment.

Just reflect for a moment on the social welfare areas receiving the most attention at this moment. Which populations, problems, and other social particulars are "in vogue" right now? In the mid–late twentieth century society at large (and thus the social work profession, in parallel) focused on aging (hence, the springing up of AARP and other organizations and systems devoted to aging with dignity). Funding for research on aging was plentiful. That area of interest waned, however, when society began to notice and focus on homelessness. And while organizations and systems arose in response to the related needs of homeless populations, less attention has been devoted to that issue of late, while culture has taken a front seat. Now it seems that everyone is talking about cultural sensitivity, cultural competence, cross-cultural understanding and appreciation.

What's next? Who knows. The point is that the kinds of social problems that get attention from society at large (and thus from our profession) shift over time, shifting as well the interest in funding related research and, in turn, shifting the context within which research is carried out as well. Political governance. Who's in office makes a difference—shifts the context. Social values and mores. The interest of high-visibility social "movers and shakers" makes a difference—shifts the context. The focus of special-interest groups (political lobbyists, potential funders, etc.) makes a difference—shifts the context. Institutional focus (nature of service, ideologies that drive mission and policies along with those of the administration, etc.) makes a difference—shifting the context even within a single institution. A broad research question may be of interest at all levels of an agency, for example, but management might inquire from a particular point of view (context), while clinical staff might be interested from another vantage point (and funders from yet another perspective). And finally, your own personal and professional world views make a difference—shifting the context of inquiry from person to person, depending on his or her professional perspective, assumptions, goals, and expectations, etc.

The context for social work research

The context for social work research that overarches all of the vagaries noted above is the profession's *Code of Ethics*, developed by the National Association of Social Workers (NASW) (www.socialworkers.org/pubs/code/default.asp) in conjunction with a set of expected "competencies" for professional social work developed by the Council on Social Work Education (EPAS, which stands for Educational Policy and Accreditation Standards) (www.cswe.org/Accreditation/2008EPAS Handbook.aspx). Together, these provide a guide (context) for both consuming and producing social work research.

The next chapter on ethics addresses the ethical guides related to research. Here, however, let's focus on the competencies most explicitly served by research:

- *Adoption of professional identity* (2.1.1): Skill in identifying, reviewing, and analyzing the professional related literature and in understanding the importance of evidence in professional social work practice (see especially Chapters 3 and 4)

- *Ethical professional conduct* (2.1.2): Ability to critique one's own practice in light of ethical mandates from the NASW *Code of Ethics*; to distinguish practices that meet professional standards from those that rest solely on tradition or "practice wisdom;" to integrate all forms of knowledge into one's approach to practice (see especially Chapter 15)
- *Skill in research-knowledge development* (2.1.6): Skill in both critiquing and applying principles and methods of problem formulation, implementation, and analysis (see especially Chapters 4 and 6); in understanding the differential application of quantitative and qualitative research (see especially Chapters 21–24); in critiquing the role and value of both types of inquiry/analysis (see especially Chapters 3, 5, and 24); in implementing independent research (see especially Chapters 6–13)
- *Developing a wider contextual view* (2.1.9): Ability to identify the potential impact of inquiry from micro (e.g., on a client system) to meso (e.g., on an agency's political structure) to macro (socio-political implications of problem formulation, implementation, and analysis); to understand the range of variables that can affect research, including contextual (researcher, setting, etc.) and political (social, cultural, economic, etc.) (see especially Chapters 2, 3, 8, and 16)
- *Skill in practice evaluation* (2.1.10): Skill in assessing everyday practice in light of professional standards and existing knowledge (i.e., professional self-assessment) and in using this process to enhance their practice (see especially Chapters 15 and 16).

Finally, do not forget that the ultimate goal of social work is to advance social welfare and justice, so that research—a form of social work practice—also inherently aims to improve practice toward an ability to affect social welfare and effect social change, not just advance knowledge for its own sake or for some abstract gain. Thus, professional ethics and accountability to these goals are important contextual considerations as we conduct a study, from selecting a question to formulate to selecting methods of implementation to considering the impact of dissemination. In the social work profession, we are mandated to go beyond a stance of doing no harm; we are mandated to actively promote well-being. At its most fundamental level, then, the context for social work research is a search for social justice, be it at the micro level (client/system empowerment), meso level (relevance of institutional mission, policies, services, etc.), or macro level (community organizing, social change, etc.).

Implications

So, what does it mean for you to approach research inquiry *in context*? It means you consider the following: the *broad social climate* in which you are going to conduct your study (or, if you are reading empirical literature, the climate in which the study you are considering was conducted); your *practice setting*—either in which or for which you are going to conduct your study (for example, institutional mission/policies/goals); and your *micro context* (the assumptions on which you operate—personal and professional world views, your values, professional expectations, self-image, biases, etc. [or those of the researchers whose work you are reviewing, as best you can discern or discover them]).

Even further, if you are engaged in either practice or program evaluation, you need to be extremely sensitive to the inherently *political* nature of research (the degree to which anyone [including you] might be invested in a particular outcome), from problem formulation (what to study and why) to analysis (the degree to which anyone [including you] might skew results consciously or subconsciously), to dissemination (receptivity to your findings). In the case of practice evaluation, the more you can approximate an experimental design, including random selection of cases to study, the less likely you are to be seen as inherently biased toward a self-congratulatory outcome. You can see this danger, right? And in the case of program evaluation, the more you can frame your study as one with potential value to all major stakeholders (rather than inherently threatening to their well-being, usually conceptualized by a system as its status quo), the more successful you will be at collecting the data you need and at having your findings incorporated by the system (in short, at not being sabotaged or wasting your time).

Major points to remember

- All science is political, conducted according to a set of assumptions about what is, what should be, and why.
- The broad context for both consuming and producing social work research is a combination of ethical mandates for the profession from NASW (see Chapter 2) and expected competencies for professional practice as identified by CSWE.
- The CSWE competencies most directly related to research are *adoption of professional identity, ethical professional conduct, skill in research-knowledge development, developing a wider contextual view,* and *skill in practice evaluation.*
- To inquire in context means to consider the broad social climate, institutional goals and expectations, and your own personal and professional assumptions, ideologies, and values.
- Practice and program evaluation demand extreme sensitivity to context so that the process is not viewed by others as inherently skewed in the former case (because you are studying yourself, inherently) or "life threatening" to the system, in the latter (threatening the status quo, often cherished by systems).
- The overarching goal of social work practice is to improve everyday quality of life; the goal of social work research is to improve the quality of social services to that end.

2

ETHICS

Key concepts

assent
benefits of participating in a research study
best practice
CITI certification
consent
informed consent
human subjects review
institutional review
instrument construction
protection of human subjects
risks of participating in a research study
vulnerable populations

Introduction

As is the case for all professions, a code of ethics governs the social work profession, and according to the National Association of Social Workers (NASW), which developed that code, the NASW *Code of Ethics* is "intended to serve as a guide to the everyday professional conduct of social workers" (www.socialworkers.org/pubs/code/default.asp). Although all components of the *Code* can be understood to pertain to all areas of practice, some language makes direct reference to the need to be *inquisitive* (i.e., to seek knowledge) and to be *competent* (i.e., to be informed). In fact, the *Code* has quite a bit to say about competence. For example, it states, "Social workers should obtain education and seek to understand the nature of social diversity and oppression with respect to race, ethnicity, national origin, color, sex, sexual orientation, gender identity or expression, age, marital status, political belief, religion, immigration status, and mental or physical disability." It also states, "Social workers continually strive to increase their professional knowledge and skills and to apply them in practice. Social workers should aspire to contribute to the knowledge base of the profession." And about education and training, the *Code* says this: "Social workers who function as educators, field instructors for students, or trainers should provide instruction … based on the most current information and knowledge available in the profession."

Finally, the *Code* devotes an entire section (5.02 *Evaluation and Research*) to research, stating (in recap form here) that social workers should: (1) evaluate all policies and practices, (2) promote practice evaluation, (3) contribute to the profession's knowledge base, (4) understand and keep current with the latest research, (5) follow guidelines to protect evaluation and research participants (clients, respondents, subjects, etc.), (6) obtain voluntary informed consent or assent (for minors) from research participants without coercion or cooptation, (7) always keep in mind the well-being of participants, (8) refrain from engaging in forms of research not based on consent protocols without explicit *a priori* approval from a review committee, (9) always let participants know they can withdraw from a study at any time without penalty, (10) ensure that participants have access to support services should they become distressed as a result of participating, (11) protect participants from unwarranted distress, (12) share findings for related professional purposes only, (13) ensure either anonymity or confidentiality of participants and of collected data (by de-identifying data), (14) report study findings accurately, (15) avoid conflicts of interest and dual relationships with participants, and (16) take measures to become educated (and to educate significant professional others) about the requirements of responsible research.

Implications

What does this all mean to you? First, it means that you should *know* (have read) and *understand the above*. If you have never done so—or if you read the NASW *Code of Ethics* some time ago (or even recently but with another "eye"), go to the website (www.socialworkers.org/pubs/code/default.asp), and read Section 5.02: *Evaluation and Research* in full. Second, it means that you *understand the implications of the above* as both a consumer and producer of research. In a nutshell, the implications are that every single person who undertakes research, whether other-directed (groups, systems, etc.) or self-directed (practice-oriented), must carefully consider that the intended study can meet all of the criteria outlined in the *Code*. Third, it means that you *explicitly integrate the above* in all aspects of your research, from problem formulation (e.g., by being able to delineate the real-world significance of a proposed study for the field) to implementation (e.g., by knowing how to go to the correct source to get the information you're after, by demonstrating your understanding of the potential risks and benefits to participants, etc.) to analysis (e.g., by paying attention to your biases during analysis, by being humble in your interpretation, by relying on evidence gathered from the study to make your interpretations, etc.) to dissemination (by offering implications for the profession in any report you develop or article you publish). Fourth, it means that you *use your practice skills to actively seek out, recognize, and consider all ways in which potential participants might feel compelled to participate*, even with what you think are gentle requests on your part.

History is replete with examples of infamous ethical infractions in social science research, and all research textbooks identify a few of them, such as the famous 40-year-long Tuskegee syphilis experiment (from the 1930s into the 1970s), the Asch conformity experiment in the 1950s, the Milgram obedience studies in the 1960s, and of course the "experiments" in twentieth-century Germany. To talk about ethics in social work research, however, is to talk not just about the potential for dramatic infractions such as these—ones that would seem obvious at anyone's first glance; it is to also talk about the small but clearly coercive power that professionals can have in dealing with people they call clients or the perspectives of power by other people (non-clients) who are invited to participate in a research study.

For example, a client might wish to please you as his or her worker or might fear some kind of reprisal, overt or otherwise, for not consenting to collaborate in practice evaluation or perhaps fear reprisal if he or she does not wish to participate in program evaluation. Such issues are not limited to clients, either. Staff members may be reluctant to participate in program evaluation for fear that what they say may somehow find its way back to management and jeopardize their job. It is essential to recognize the impact of this inherent power differential (service provider/receiver or researcher/staff member, etc.) along with the potential impact of cultural factors (norms, values, traditions, expectations, etc.) on people's views about and histories with research, on their understanding of their relationship with service providers such as social workers, and on their perceptions of possible risks from collaborating.

One of the major ways in which we can attend to ethics in research is by making sure we create and implement a protocol for *informed consent*, a concept that applies to social work practice in all its forms, not just research. In fact, informed consent is a fundamental value of the profession generally, meaning, all things equal, that people with whom we come into professional contact for service or treatment understand and agree to the nature of that contact. In short, we do not do "to" or "at" people but, rather, "with" people. Service or treatment is, to all feasible extent, collaborative; and if it cannot be so for any reason, then we need enormous justification for acting without the full cooperation of the client/system. Here are some ethical mandates related to informed consent in general social work practice from Section 1.03 of the NASW *Code of Ethics*, which is available online: "Social workers should receive informed consent for services... be clear in informing clients about purposes of services and possible related risks and limits... let clients know about rights of refusal and alternatives... provide opportunities for questions/do whatever is necessary to ensure comprehension... protect clients' interests as necessary… (and) obtain informed consent before recording clients in any way or recording interactions with clients" (www.socialworkers.org/pubs/code/default.asp for the full language).

Finally, it means that in most cases—and particularly in cases that rely on federal funding—researchers must take a CITI Program Human Subject Protection continuing-education course (see more on this below). In a nutshell, then, informed consent is integral to social work ethics, and in the rare case when consent is not feasible, *a priori* approval from an institutionally based human-subjects review committee [see below]).

From idea to action: integrating informed consent into research

Today, as a result of many infractions over the years, the concept of *protection for human subjects* is integral to social work research. What this refers to is simply this— that anyone who participates in a research project is entitled to be protected from any potential harm as a result of his or her participation and, further, should any risks to his or her well-being be possible, is made aware of those risks so that his or her consent to participate is truly informed. Today, almost every institution that engages in research has a human-subjects review board (sometimes referred to as an institutional review board), a committee of persons (research experts) charged with the role of reviewing research proposals from members of that institution and with the responsibility of approving or withholding approval in accordance with professional ethical mandates noted above.

Applications for approval of a study to such boards must include an overview of the study's purpose; discuss its significance to the profession (usually through a brief overview of the related literature); describe and justify its proposed design; describe in detail its proposed methods, including sampling procedures and data collection protocols; and include every document to be utilized in the study (recruitment materials, the instrument/s to be used, etc.) including an *Informed Consent* form with much boilerplate language made specific to that particular study. Proceeding with implementation without approval is an egregious offense.

The Informed Consent *form*

The *Informed Consent* form is either signed by the participant or in some other way acknowledged, such as online studies, in which participants do not sign and return a form but acknowledge their understanding and acceptance of the study's parameters as outlined in an *Informed Consent* form (page) by "clicking" on a button that takes them to the survey, for example. It generally includes an *introduction*, which explains why the person reading the form is being asked to do so (e.g., *You are being asked to participate in a study that will …*), describes the *context of the study* (its purpose and procedures), identifies *possible risks and benefits of participating* (including such risks as distress from self-reflection or reflection about a particular state of affairs and such benefits as the satisfaction that comes with helping to advance knowledge usually in an area of interest to that person), and describes *conditions of confidentiality or anonymity*. Also identified on the form is whether the potential respondent can expect any *payments or gifts* (or other types of tangible rewards), a statement about his or her *rights of refusal or withdrawal* (even after agreeing to participate) without penalty, and a statement about his or her *right to ask questions* about any and/or all aspects of the study (or the informed consent protocol) along with contact information for both the researcher and the institution under the auspices of which the research is taking place.

The form ends with a declaration by the potential respondent that he or she *understands and agrees to the terms* proposed in the consent form and *consents to participate*. Further, if recording of any kind may be involved, there is a separate statement at the end of the form about the *nature of the recording*, and the respondent has the choice to select agreement to be recorded or not. This means that someone might be willing to participate in an interview, for example, and still withhold the right of the researcher to audio or video record that interview. Finally, depending on the nature of subjects being sought for the study, the consent may have an attachment outlining a number of *free or low-cost resources for post-study counseling*, should it be needed.

Consent versus assent

Informed consent refers to the voluntary agreement of an individual (or authorized representative) to give consent freely, without coercion or constraint, to participate in a study. He or she must understand the nature of the study, anticipated risks and potential benefits, and what is expected of him or her in order to make an *informed* decision.

Assent refers to the willingness to participate by someone who is by definition too young (a "child" or "minor") to give informed consent but who is still old enough to understand the purpose of the research, along with risks, benefits, expectations, etc. Assent must be always accompanied by informed consent from a guardian, however, so that assent alone is never enough to proceed with data collection. Who constitutes a "child" or "minor" varies from state to state.

Vulnerable populations

Federal regulations require that review boards give special consideration to protecting the well-being of particularly vulnerable populations, which they define as follows: children/minors (under 18); prisoners; pregnant women; mentally or physically disabled persons (including cognitively impaired or institutionalized elderly); and economically or educationally disadvantaged persons. Generally, review boards will approve studies with such populations as long as the risks of participating are minimal.

The CITI program

To help ensure that researchers are aware of their many professional and ethical obligations, a training and education program was instituted in 2000—the CITI Program. CITI stands for Collaborative Institutional Training Initiative, and based at the University of Miami in Florida, the CITI Program trains people all over the world through the World Wide Web in research history, protocols, and ethics for many different fields, including social work. Its mission statement, readily available on its website (www.citiprogram.org) is as follows:

> To promote the public's trust in the research enterprise by providing high quality, peer reviewed, web based, research education materials to enhance the integrity and professionalism of investigators and staff conducting research.

The CITI Program is composed of many expert writers, editors, and reviewers who create training content in a wide range of areas including but not limited to animal research, biosafety, clinical practice, human-subjects research, information privacy, responsible research conduct, and conflict of interest. CITI training is considered a national "best practice" for anyone involved with research and is generally expected of all investigators and related personnel, including those who design the study, implement the study, analyze data, or report the findings. CITI certification is good for a three-year period, after which the certification must be renewed, ensuring that researchers keep up with the latest ethical mandates.

A note on the ethics of instrument design

There are two ways to conceptualize instrument design—that is, what should be included in a questionnaire or on an interview guide, for example. On the one hand, we want to collect as much data as possible—not only just enough to answer the question but also enough to provide our consumers with contextual information, i.e., about the sample and its characteristics. Without context (who responded), findings are less than meaningful. Only when we understand the context within which research findings are offered can we make meaning of (apply) them. On the other hand, however, it is not ethical to ask for information that is not directly related/pertinent to the research question. While review boards do examine proposed instruments closely and hopefully catch items that appear to be either somewhat incongruous with or superfluous to the study, it still behooves the researcher to consider the necessity and relevance of each and every single item in whatever data collection method is to be used.

You need to give some serious thought, then, to not only *how* you construct your items but *why* each one is included, as well. It is tempting to try to learn as much as possible, knowing that this study is your "in" to the area of interest—your (perhaps once-in-a-lifetime) opportunity to glean as much as possible, especially given all the work you have put into launching the study in the first place. *If I do not ask this, will I regret it later*, you wonder … *I better ask it now, just in case*. Of course, respondents can always refuse to answer any given question/item on a questionnaire (assuming they are doing so in private), but that is beside the point here. The point is that unless you have a valid reason to ask for a particular piece of information—a reason that is clearly related to the study's purpose and that you could justify if challenged—you shouldn't ask it.

Major points to remember

* Social work research is governed by the same NASW *Code of Ethics* that governs general social work practice.
* Responsible research begins with knowing and understanding the *Code of Ethics* and understanding its implications for both consuming and producing research.
* Responsible research also means explicit integration of ethical principles into all aspects of a research study, from problem formulation to dissemination, including considering ways in which potential participants might feel coerced (or coopted) to participate/afraid to say no.
* A major way of attending to ethics in social work research is to make sure we create and implement a protocol for *informed consent*.
* Today, most researchers are required to become certified (and to renew certification every three years) by the Collaborative Institutional Training Initiative (CITI), a continuing-education training course, available world-wide online.
* Most institutions that engage in research have human-subjects review boards, charged with reviewing research proposals and approving or withholding approval in accordance with professional ethical mandates.
* Applications for approval of a proposed study include an overview of its purpose; a statement about professional significance; and details about design, methods, and materials to be used including an *Informed Consent* form.
* *Informed consent* refers to the voluntary agreement to participate in a study. *Assent* refers to the voluntary agreement by someone who is still a child or minor (as defined by each state). Assent never stands alone; it must be accompanied by a guardian's informed consent.
* Some populations (see earlier) are considered vulnerable, and, generally, review boards will approve studies with such populations as long as the risks of participating are minimal.
* In constructing a research instrument, it is important to reflect on the nature and necessity of each item, balancing the desire for knowledge with respect for people's privacy. This means that if an item is simply of interest but not particularly relevant to the study's purpose, leave it off.

3

EVIDENCE AND PROFESSIONAL SOCIAL WORK PRACTICE

Key concepts

being informed
case/client context
code of ethics
evidence
evidence-based practice/s
information literacy
information literacy skills
professionalism
purposes of evidence
tradition/authority

Introduction

All informed action requires evidence, and in social work acting from a stance of informed action is what separates the professional from the nonprofessional (or *technician* or *friendly visitor/good Samaritan*), images that the profession has been trying to move away from for over 100 years. In the courtroom, evidence is key in determining the outcome of a trial, the results of which can mean life or death for someone. In medicine it is equally important, and we would not wish the medical world to treat us on any other basis. Can you imagine what health care would look like if psychiatrists, for example, just continued year after year to practice and prescribe according only to theoretical knowledge or tradition or authority (what has always been done or what we say goes)? Well, professional social work has as much potential (if not more in many cases) to do harm as good, and it is imperative that our actions be *informed*—informed by many factors. And to become informed means to *understand case context*, to *apply professional insight*, and to *pay attention to the newest related research*. The question, then, is not *if* evidence-based practice is worthwhile but *how* to dissect and understand the value of all forms of knowledge and integrate them into practice so that practice is truly informed.

Evidence: what is it?

The concept of evidence—despite being the "sexy" concept in the literature today—presents many a conundrum to even seasoned practitioners. Defining it is neither easy nor clear-cut. In the context of this subject, you might say that conceptually, we all "get" it; to define it operationally, however, is another matter altogether.

In effect, most professional social workers agree that *evidence-based practice* refers to a way of working with people we call clients that relies on the integration of information from (1) the client/case context (attending to the "here and now," often formally referred to as attending to "person in environment"); (2) knowledge about what treatment/service has been (so far) "tried and true" for such (or similar) cases (often referred to as tradition, authority, or practice wisdom); and (3) the ever-evolving body of empirical research about the type of client/case in question or about related clients/cases.

Clients usually bring complex problems to social work, however, and their right to self-determination must be respected, so that integrating the three areas of consideration noted above poses several challenges. We cannot simply review and apply available empirical information (or practice wisdom, for that matter) to a client's situation even if we consider his or her unique characteristics. Rather, we are required by the National Association of Social Workers *Code of Ethics* (www.socialworkers.org/pubs/code/default.asp) to engage in a complex collaborative decision-making process to determine a best course of action, a process that is far easier said than done. We must integrate many variables to achieve solutions that are truly effective, a process that becomes increasingly complex as cultures, values, and world views collide ever more intensely. In the end, what's most important is that we agree to look in every crevice for possible enlightenment so that we can, in fact, do more good than harm—that we do not say, for example, *Oh, I don't care to read the new research! It doesn't apply to me* or *Oh, I can't understand that lingo, so I'm just going to stay as far away from it as possible*. Those positions reflect the antithesis of professional practice. In fact, to rely on what has been "always done" or "So and so says to do it this way" is, according to our *Code of Ethics*, unethical.

Meaning and implications

Evidence serves different purposes in practice; it can be exploratory, descriptive, experimental, or correlational in nature (see Chapters 10–13). It can, for example, (1) turn the light on something that has been in relative darkness, showing us that something's going on here and helping us to formulate questions; this is an "exploratory"-oriented purpose; (2) turn that light up more brightly on something that we know is going on but aren't quite sure what, so we look more closely and begin to better understand the nuances of what we're looking at; this is a "descriptive" purpose; (3) target a particular piece of that puzzle to help us look more closely at the possibility of relationships among factors (that perhaps we had not considered); this would be "correlational" evidence; and finally (4) help us to turn our focus from looking at possible relationships among factors to look even more closely at the possibility that the presence of one of those factors is actually causing another to exist; this would be "experimental" evidence. To engage in any of these purposes requires you to have *information literacy* skills, which means skill in the following:

1   ability to determine what and how much information you need;
2   ability to access whatever information you believe you need;
3   ability to critically evaluate the applicability of the information you do access within the context of professional ethics and values;
4   ability to integrate new information you see as relevant, valuable, and ethical into your approach to practice.

Going about evidence-based practice (EBP) research

There are two general approaches to EBP research. One is that experts—generally researchers, policy makers, and academics—carry out the research and translate their findings into specific practices for workers to learn and carry out (a kind of deductive or "top-down" approach). The other is that workers or agencies take responsibility for developing questions (a kind of inductive or "bottom-up" approach) based on a particular client/case problem and desire for a specific outcome (e.g., reduced recidivism). Both approaches call for sharing what is learned with the client or client system in order to consider specific context, values, needs, and goals in developing subsequent treatment or service plans.

Methods (steps) in EBP research

EBP research methods consist of the following steps:

1   developing a relevant practice question;
2   locating, systematically reviewing, and synthesizing related empirical research;
3   making decisions together with the client system in question about how to use all the information available.

As you can see, EBP has a lot of commonality with practice in general: we collect information from our client/system in order to identify all the issues, problems, and goals that bring us into contact; we collect all available knowledge related to what we have discovered in order to develop a treatment/service plan; and we bring all we know back to the client/system in order to implement a plan that satisfies all the stakeholders (client/system, the worker within the context of professional-practice mandates, and the agency/setting mission/policies).

Practice vs. practices: what's in a word?

Are you confused about evidence-based practice versus evidence-based practices? Don't worry! You are not alone. There seems to be a great deal of confusion when people talk about evidence as it pertains to practice. That's because there are two "animals" to talk about: evidence-based *practice* and evidence-based *practices*. Here is a nutshell about each one.

Evidence-based practice

Evidence-based practice (practice, singular) refers to the broad approach or process, you might say, to your work. It connotes your professional world view, if you will, about how to be an effective practitioner (that is, the best you can be). Thus, evidence-based practice means an approach to practice that relies on the integration of empirical study about the work/problem area with theory, tradition (what has always been done, if it applies, logically and ethically), and authority (tried and true, practice wisdom, etc., including your own insights gleaned from practice), and the context (needs, goals, values, etc.) of the client system/case in question.

According to the Council on Social Work Education (www.cswe.org), the five important steps in evidence-based practice are as follows:

1 formulating a client-, community-, or policy-related question;
2 systematically searching the literature;
3 appraising findings for quality and applicability;
4 applying these findings and considerations in practice;
5 evaluating the results.

Thus, if you are an evidence-based practitioner, you engage in these steps whenever you practice, whether it is working with an individual client, a group system, or a community (such as community organizing); engaging in program evaluation (such as, an inquiry about organizational practices); or even developing new program policies or protocols.

Evidence-based practices

In contrast, evidence-based *practices* refer to treatment/service methods (interventions) for which there is scientific evidence (that is, evidence that they improve outcomes for clients/systems [or programmatic outcomes, if that is the target system of interest]). Three examples of evidence-based practices well known to social work are *eye movement desensitization and reprocessing* (EMDR), *dialectical behavior therapy* (DBT), and *motivational interviewing* (MI). For an enormous roster of evidence-based practices, check out the SAMHSA National Registry of Evidence-Based Programs and Practice (NREBP) website (http://www.samhsa.gov/nrepp).

Be sure, then, in any dialogue with other professionals that you distinguish between these two definitions (concepts) as they relate to practice. One (practice, singular) connotes a professional process consisting of particular steps to identify and implement particular interventions, steps that include consideration (1) of available empirical evidence related to the problem/issue in question, (2) of client/case context, and (3) of service context (agency mission, etc.). The other (practices, plural) refers to specific interventions that are empirically supported in terms of their ability to improve client/case outcomes.

Major points to remember

- The concept of evidence is important to social work practice, separating the Good Samaritan from the professional, who relies on evidence rather than surmise, theory, or tradition to make treatment/service decisions.
- Evidence-based *practice* (EBP) refers to an approach to social work that integrates empirical evidence with client/case context (including client needs, goals, and values) and agency/setting (mission/policies) in developing treatment/service plans. Evidence-based *practices* refer to specific interventions for which there is scientific evidence that they improve outcomes.
- To ignore empirical evidence related to a client/case of interest is, according to the NASW *Code of Ethics*, unethical behavior.
- Integrating empirical evidence into practice leads to *informed* practice, a hallmark of professionalism.
- Evidence can serve different purposes in practice. In parallel with purposes of research, it can be exploratory (shed new light), descriptive (offer better details), correlational (suggest heretofore unnoticed possible associations), or experimental (propose the possibility of a logical causal relationship).
- To engage in any of the purposes noted above requires *information literacy* skills, which are generally the ability to determine what/how much information you need to create a service/treatment plan; the ability to access whatever information you believe you need; the ability to critically evaluate the applicability of the information you do access within the context of professional ethics and values; and the ability to integrate new information you see as relevant, valuable, and ethical into your approach to practice.
- EBP research methods are similar to those of practice, consisting of developing a relevant practice question; locating, systematically reviewing, and synthesizing related empirical research; and making decisions together with the client system in question about how to use all the information available.

4

PROBLEM FORMULATION: WHAT TO STUDY

(Getting started)

Key concepts

back-and-forth thinking
felt difficulties
focus
inquiry
internal versus external motivation
pleading a cause
problem
problem formulation
problem identification
professional significance

Selecting a study topic

Moving through the funnel

Time to select a study topic? Interested in many areas? Like to know more about all of them? Then it's time to begin problem identification, Part 1 of problem formulation. Part 2 of the process takes the same title as the whole process, problem formulation. Problem identification is the search for a general area of interest that has professional meaning. As Part 2 of the process, problem formulation is the articulation of a research problem in statement form that says what you mean and means what you really want it to say.

So, what's a research problem?

In research lingo the term *problem* has no negative connotation. We could just as well use *issue, concern, dilemma, question,* or even *gap in knowledge* that needs exploration, examination, or resolution.

Let's say you're invited to two holiday dinners at once. You have a problem, yes … but boy oh boy, what a wonderful problem! So don't begin this process with a negative mindset. Your research problem is simply the specific topic that you choose to study. So a problem for research is some indeterminate state of affairs in the universe that you believe needs "closure." When you can articulate it, you will have articulated your problem statement (i.e., what's wrong with something that you want to "fix" through scientifically based study).

Once you have a general idea about that state of affairs, you are ready to engage in the more challenging process of problem formulation. Yes, you've identified the problem area, but now you need to articulate it very concisely in both thought and word.

Mindset

Think of this process, problem formulation, as a funnel through which your thinking must pass (Figure 4.1). You can see that there's a lot more space at the top than the bottom, right? That's because you begin this process by playing around with ideas, by brainstorming, by examining lots of different possible areas to explore, to study, to learn about. Here, you are just looking around in the universe, sensing that all is not right.

So you begin with a good long stretch of sitting at the top rim as you ponder a broad area of interest to you (*problem identification* i.e., identifying a general research problem), maybe taking one step downward and then back up as new ideas and possibilities open up through reading, thinking, and talking with others. Then, as your thinking becomes increasingly refined, you continue down to the narrowest part of the funnel, each step representing further conceptual focus until you can articulate the problem (as a hypothesis or question) clearly and specifically enough to pass completely through the neck.

As you do this, a few things will happen. You may discover that there's more information on your topic than you realized and that it answers some or even many of your questions. In that case, you may find that new questions develop, even making you more rather than less confused about what to study. Uh oh! Don't get upset! Remember how to eat an elephant? One bite at a time. Or how to attack a problem? One piece at a time. Here, your mantra is *read, think, talk, rest, read, think, talk, rest* … things will come together.

It's okay if your thinking goes back and forth and back and forth; bit by bit it's advancing the process. Research has a lot of swing to it! But every bit of thinking and rethinking brings you closer to clarity and focus. So, it may well be that as you travel this particular funnel, you'll defy gravity by occasionally jumping back up a

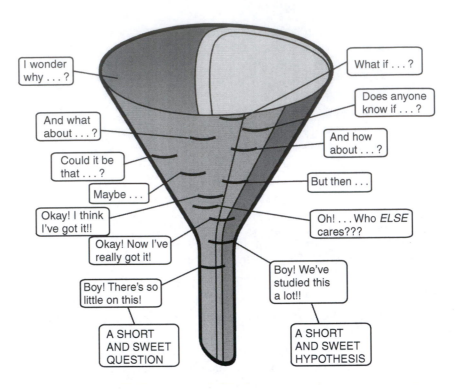

FIGURE 4.1 Problem formulation funnel

step or two to regroup, to change your interest or perspective ever so slightly and then start back down again. But back-and-forth thinking is a norm, not a failure of good decision making. In fact, expect it, accept it, and even embrace it! Much of the stuff of problem formulation is playing around with ideas, with revisiting and revision being part and parcel of the journey. You'll do a lot of this in practice, too! There's not too much linear thinking or action in social work!

Uh ... you're not secretly trying to plead a cause, right?

Sometimes people get stuck in this process because they already have ideas that they really want to get across to others—to write a position paper, to promote a treasured belief. That mindset, however, makes it absolutely impossible for you to remain in a questioning mode, which is where you're supposed to be. So remember, this part of research is all and only about developing a question, not how to get an answer (your values, beliefs, attitudes, assumptions, or desires) across to others. The guiding principle here is: *formulate a study that actually studies!*

Can you live with any result?

Whatever hypothesis you eventually want to test or question you want to answer, you need to think about the acceptability of potential results. Will it be all right with you if you carry out a study and the results suggest that all things are not what you thought them to be? Perhaps your approach to practice is less effective than you hoped ... Or what if results tell you things that are contrary to your values or expectations—surprising in some way? Or not all that pleasant to your ego, for example? If that is okay, if you can accept that, then go ahead and study that topic, ask that question, test that hypothesis. But be honest with yourself. If you can imagine that some findings would be really difficult for you to live with, find another topic.

Who but you cares about this study?

Oh? Now you're worried that your questions are only interesting to you and not as brilliant as, say, those of Albert Einstein or even those of your peers? Don't worry! In fact, research is rarely cosmic in scope; and the point here isn't to create an éclat. Don't get caught up in *bigger is better*. The point is to gain a piece of knowledge that will be of real and practical use to your everyday work. Maybe that's knowing more about how veteran practitioners incorporate certain cognitive tasks into their practice with addiction; maybe it's a closer look at a group treatment program; maybe it's an updated description of agency cases so that you can represent the agency better in your next funding proposal; maybe it's an exploration of current difficulties in a refugee camp; and on and on ad infinitum. If you can argue for the utility of prospective findings to social work, then you have a legitimate pursuit.

Motivation: internal versus external impetus

On the other hand ... not every form of inquiry is research. Some is therapy. Yes, we often develop professional interest in areas that hit close to home; but here's the rub for research. If our impetus is strictly internal (some call it navel gazing), then we're bound to engage in therapy rather than research. How does that look? For one thing, you'll have difficulty designing an instrument (e.g., an interview guide) with professional distance. Then you'll lose any semblance of professional interest in the project as soon as your question is answered on your personal behalf. Third, your biases will weigh heavily upon your data analysis. And finally, you may simply become stuck—unable to complete the process because the content (literature, data collected, results, etc.) is personally overwhelming.

Now what?

If you feel confident about carrying on in your selected direction, now's the time to work toward balance between developing a problem that's of interest only to you and one that's too cosmic and unrealistic to pursue. How so? Don't go at it alone! Talk to friends, teachers, and colleagues—anyone who's interested and will listen! Problem formulation is rarely if ever carried out alone. The image of a lonely white coat tucked away in a lab testing a theory no one else knows about doesn't pertain to social science research. Rather, think of this process as brainstorming, and, like all such processes, the rule of thumb is *the more the merrier*! In fact, one of the best ways to know if you're clear in your thinking and on target is when others in the know tell you so.

Lots to think about? Of course! That's what makes this the most difficult part of the process! But it can also be much fun, playing around with possibilities.

Ask yourself

1 *What do I want to know? What are some professional issues of interest to me—an unanswered question, some gap in my knowledge?* You might begin by deciding if you're interested primarily in practice (conceptual approach, method, model, impact of national policies, etc.) or population (practitioners, women, children, homeless persons, nursing home residents, people hospitalized for a certain illness, etc.) or problem (issues of education, addiction, teen pregnancy, attachment, resilience, mental illness, etc.).

2 Now get more specific within the context of your response to Question 1. *What more particular issues am I interested in?* Social work practice in medical settings? The nature of professional education? Statistics on homelessness? Issues that confront homeless persons who seek work? Alcoholism among the elderly? Grief work in treatment with addicted persons? The history of "work fare" legislation? The impact of current legislation on single-parent households? Day treatment programs for cognitively impaired persons? Treatment approaches for working with sexually abused adolescents?

3 *Now, what difference would the study of this issue make to social work?* On what area of practice? On direct service? On social work education? On the potential for social action? Then, ask yourself who else would be interested in such a study? Remember, even with personal interest, your question must be of professional utility. If you can identify concrete ways in which the results could be used by other professionals, you're on your way.

4 Finally, ask yourself, *Can I live with all possible results?* Yes? Great. That means your mind is open to true inquiry. Not sure? Do more thinking. And be honest; you'll save yourself lots of angst later.

Major points to remember

• Social work research mandates implications for practice, recommendations for helping us do what we do better.

- Problem formulation has two steps. Identification refers to your broad topic area; formulation refers to the angle from which you're going to examine that area.
- At the end of this process you will have developed research problem stated in either a hypothesis or question form and stated simply enough to repeat over and over again from memory.
- Don't assign a negative connotation to the term "research problem." A research problem simply represents some gap in knowledge that needs to be "closed" (resolved) through inquiry, close examination, and analysis.
- Think of problem formulation as descending a funnel starting with a good long stretch on top as you identify a broad area of interest and moving down through its neck, each step representing further conceptual refinement.
- A research problem is not how to get an answer you already have across to others; it's your idea of a felt difficulty out there in the universe, some gap in our professional knowledge that needs answering.
- All potential results of a research study must be acceptable, whether they confirm, disconfirm, surprise, or disappoint.
- Research is rarely cosmic in scope; the point is to gain a piece of knowledge that will be of real and practical use.
- Not every form of inquiry is research. Some is therapy. In research, the felt difficulty to be examined is external; in therapy, the felt difficulty to be examined is internal.

Exercise

Test yourself

Repeat your research hypothesis or question five times without looking at the paper on which it's written. Can you do it? Remember: the more simply stated, the more it will keep you on track.

Once you can do that, articulate your research problem to others. Choose peers who are likely to understand some degree of research (co-students, teachers, supervisors, advisors, etc.). If they understand what you mean, you are probably clear. If they keep asking, if they are confused, or if they do not seem to understand what you're trying to get at, you have probably not refined your statement well enough yet. Keep working on it. Get to a point at which you say what you mean, and you mean what you say.

5

USING THE LITERATURE

(Who has said what about this already?
So what?)

Key concepts

accountability
context
critiquing
discussion
focus
heartbeat
organization
reading around
related literature
relatedness
reporting
reviewing

Introduction

There is a logical relationship between what's already known about your topic (as reflected by the literature) and the way you ultimately formulate your research problem. You can't know the nature of that relationship, however, until you've reviewed that literature. Your understanding of this relationship begins with a search for all the work, conceptual and empirical, that pertains to your area of interest; and it culminates in a written review that presents, discusses, analyzes, and critiques that work and connects it to the rationale for your own work.

Part 1: The search

Mindset

The mindset for the search is one of trying to make yourself "intelligent." Once you select a general topic and search out what others have said or done about it, you gain the knowledge and insight to formulate a problem intelligently. Then, by reviewing that literature in written form, you provide both a foundation and context for your own work and make your consumers intelligent as well. Only when they understand how your work fits into the overall picture, both historically and contemporaneously, can they assess the meaning and impact of your results.

Reading around

A lot to think about? Absolutely! And the way to begin is by "reading around." Start with social work literature, since your study is in, of, and for the benefit of that field. Then, move on to other bodies of literature that may speak to your topic, such as psychology and education—even medicine, religion, philosophy, politics, economics, and probably others. You might look in popular literature, too, such as newspapers and magazines both off- and online. Ultimately, you may find that more than one body of literature speaks to your subject.

The goal here? To read enough to be able to formulate and then articulate the purpose of your study in a sentence that truly reflects what you want to know and is simple enough to repeat over and over again without looking at it in writing! The secondary goal is to read enough to feel comfortable defending your study. *No, this phenomenon has never been examined before (and I am comfortable saying this in my proposal for study, because I have reviewed the literature, direct and related)*. Or *Yes, it has been examined but with another population* (or in another setting or geographic area, etc.). Or (and this is often the case) *Yes, it has been examined but only cursorily, as an exploratory study, and now I would like to examine it differently* (in greater depth or with a different method, e.g., from a large-scale descriptive approach, and thus slightly different purpose).

Maybe your statement of study will have a period after it, in which case you'll work from now on to test a hypothesis, because a hypothesis is a declaratory statement: *I believe this (and am going to test that belief)*. You see how that warrants a period at the end? Or maybe it will end with a question mark, in which case you'll work to answer a question. Why a question? Basically because you cannot get yourself, even after reading all the related literature, to a point at which you feel confident to formulate a hypothesis, which is essentially an educated hunch about something (state of affairs, dynamic, relationship, etc.). Exploratory studies are often formulated using a question, for example. (For more on hypotheses and questions, see Chapter 6.)

Going about it the right way

What goes into a good search? Start by seeking the most current material (usually in professional journals) and work backward. And be sure to search their bibliographies for leads. Then move to books, encyclopedias, and, for contemporary events, newspaper indices. Don't overlook *Bibliographic Index*, *Bibliography of Bibliographies*, and similar standard reference sources. Some catalogs are useful to locate books as well, such as the *Cumulative Book Index* and *Books in Print*. Library of Congress services like Medlars, ERIC, and University Microfilms may also be useful. And of course, search the World Wide Web for literature from professional and popular databases, public libraries, and public and private organizations and associations.

Be sure to search for and emphasize literature that presents empirical studies on your topic. These are the research studies that have already looked at your area of interest from one angle or another. The last thing you want to do is spend all this time developing a research study only to discover, accidentally, that your question was already asked and answered—but you didn't know it, because you didn't search the existing research. In addition to searching generally, there are special sources where you can look for this kind of literature, such as Cochrane Reviews and Campbell Systematic Reviews. Both of these, which you will find on the internet, present just the kind of empirical studies in the health and human service fields that can help propel your own study forward. In every area you explore, be sure to look for any existing research—reports, articles, books, etc.—that examined your area *or a related area* of interest.

When is it enough?

"Enough" reading around is when you find that wherever you look you run into titles of books and articles you've read already. In other words, you've pretty much saturated the literature on your topic. Of course, "the literature" is not static! No sooner do you finish an article than another is in press. In real-world terms, then, "enough" is when you think you know enough about the subject to develop a clear and focused study, design a reliable and valid instrument, and develop a sound data collection plan. Might there yet be a piece of literature you've not read as you implement your study? Sure. There's always more to read. But that's okay. If you have a chance to read and integrate a new piece of literature later on, fine. If not, it will go into the next study, be it yours or someone else's.

"Use" it or lose it

Valuable references are often encountered unexpectedly. If you don't want to carry index cards around, create a file on your laptop that includes for everything you read (1) its author, (2) its title, (3) its publisher, and (4) relevant pages. Then jot down (5) its source, (6) how that piece of literature relates to your problem, (7) how it might be used in your review (often one piece of literature is used several times in a review, which is organized by theme and thus may touch on any given piece of literature in several ways), and (8) any other commentary you think is important at that time. Be sure to critique, not just describe, what the literature says.

Always keep in mind your hypothesis or question as you read (even if you are in the process of formulating it; at least keep in mind your research problem—that gap in the universe you are interested in closing for yourself), reminding yourself how, exactly, it fits into what you're doing. And mark that on your card or at the top of your file list of sources. This will help prevent collecting a huge but haphazard and useless bibliography You might also make copies of the literature, cut out those sections that pertain to various themes, and collect them in paper bags, stored in your closet, marked with the title of each theme. This very low-tech approach offers a comprehensive at-a-glance view of how and where different pieces of literature fit into your overall proposal (or report).

Part 2: Writing the review

Mindset

Think of this section as a discussion with a friend about what others have said and found on your subject. And just as you would offer commentary in that discussion, be sure that the reader can sense your own heartbeat in the review, i.e., what you think about what has been said and done.

Have a plan

Begin with a tentative outline of major points to see if they make sense, to see how to best organize their presentation (what logically comes before what), to check for holes (what needs to be beefed up), to check for redundancy (where it can be tightened), even to see if sections should be combined. Then use that outline to create as many headings and subheadings as needed to keep the conceptual flow clear, both for you and the reader. Note: it's better to reduce too many headings than to make readers wade through long sections with no guidance. Remember, your purpose is to set the stage for your own study, to present your rationale and context for the work you have (in a proposal) or had (in a report) in mind. Also remember that more is not necessarily more in this context. More is all about clear organization and flow, including conceptual connections that help the reader understand why you are saying what you are saying.

Writing

Think in terms of an hourglass for each section and subsection. Begin from a comprehensive view with broad introductory statements; then move to specifics with details (explanation, clarification, expansion, etc.) and examples; finally, close with a broad summary statement and a conceptual transition to the next section.

Begin with classic literature, the earliest or most well-known thinking, writing, and research that has paved the way for your own work. The efforts of "trailblazers" provide a historic context, a conceptual lineage to current thinking. Then move to contemporaneous efforts to understand your topic (thinking, research, etc.)

Emphasize relatedness: be accountable

Remember to keep your reader constantly aware of how the literature relates to your own study. Account for each study or any article/piece of literature you cite by pointing out specifically its relationship to your research problem. Don't leave your readers hanging, wondering why you're talking about it. Make the connections clear. Unless you can establish such accountability, you'd do well to not use that piece of literature at all. And don't be afraid of repetition. Remember that the reader doesn't have the same material in his or her head. You don't want the reader to try to understand on his or her own why one sentence is following another. Conceptual bridges are crucial and are often created through such terms as *For example*, *However*, *Consequently*, etc. (see a list at the end of this chapter). Finally, don't forget to make proper citations for pieces of literature to which you refer, including page reference for (*and only for*) direct quotes.

Integrate your heartbeat (what you think)

Finally, don't write a chain of pointless isolated summaries of other people's writing or thinking, such as *Jones says ... Smith says ... Green says*, etc. This is not a review; it's a report. The difference? A review reflects your heartbeat—what you think about what others have said and done, why it's important to your study. In other words, it demonstrates the relatedness of the literature to your research problem. A report is simply a description without analysis or critique.

Major points to remember

- Searching the literature on your topic makes it possible to develop an "intelligent" research question.
- A good search begins by "reading around" in the body of literature most pertinent to your topic and then expanding to consider other possibly related literature, both professional and popular.
- Most important to include in your literature search is all of the empirical work already conducted in your area of interest, both directly and indirectly (either

in related fields or on related problems in your field). This places your proposed study in context.

- The goal of a search is to read enough to be able to articulate your research problem as a question or hypothesis.
- A search begins with current material and works backward. It includes articles, books, encyclopedias, catalogs, bibliographies, and even popular literature and web-based material.
- "Enough" is when you run into titles of books and articles you've read already.
- Always carry a few index cards to jot down unexpected references.
- Think of the written review of the literature as a discussion with a friend about what others have said and found on your subject.
- Use an outline to organize your review and create headings and subheadings to keep the conceptual flow of your discussion clear.
- Begin discussions from a comprehensive perspective, move to specifics, and close with broad summary and transitional statements.
- Keep your reader aware of how each piece of literature relates to your study. Account for each study you cite. Don't write a chain of pointless isolated summaries of other people's writing or thinking.

Exercises

Self-Assessment 1

As you read around, ask yourself these questions with regard to your topic area:

1 *How does my thinking fit into the general picture, both historically and contemporaneously?*
2 *How does my formulation compare to those of previous studies on this topic?*
3 *Does the literature suggest a consensus of thought on my topic, or are there some important controversies, debates, or divergences? If so, what kind of contribution would my study make?*

Self-Assessment 2

1 Free write what you think you know about your topic. Don't pay too much attention to form and grammar, etc. Instead, focus on the substance.
2 Read over what you've written and pick out major themes. What does the history of your topic look like? How did social work come to pay attention to it? Or has it even done so? Perhaps other fields have explored it more than social work. If so, say so, and reflect on the topic from those perspectives. Who are important figures—scholars, researchers, advocates, etc.? How have they contributed to our current understanding? So what's happening today? The thinking? The research? And what's missing, in your opinion? What's your understanding of the current gap in knowledge?

Answering these questions will help you develop a formal outline that expands what you've already written and, in that expansion, help you to make a case for your study.

Some useful conceptual connectors in writing

For example,	However,	if, and, or, but
Therefore,	Be that as it may,	In as much as
Thus,	Hence,	Consequently,
To the extent that	Furthermore,	Finally,
In summary,	In short,	Nevertheless,
Still,	Yet,	In contrast,
On the other hand,	Naturally,	Evidently,
Fortunately,	Curiously enough,	As previously noted,
Ultimately,	Eventually,	Moreover,
Likewise,	Accordingly,	Generally speaking,
More specifically,	Especially noteworthy is …	As noted earlier,
First, …	Second, …	Third, …

Exceptions notwithstanding, … ? (Can you add others)

You will find more about writing for publication in Steinberg, D. M. (2007). "From Pen to Paper: Passing on Some Tips," in *Social Work with Groups* (30)2, 41–55.

Acknowledgement

Special thanks to Dr. Roselle Kurland for her literature review notes and handouts so many years ago.

6

WORKING FROM QUESTIONS OR HYPOTHESES

(To ask or to test? That is the question)

Key concepts

conjecture
hypothesis
null hypothesis
proof
question
refutation
substantiation

Introduction

Should you work from a question or develop a hypothesis? Don't try to decide before other things come into clearer sight; there's a logical relationship between existing knowledge on your topic (which you have learned or are in the process of learning by reviewing the literature) and how you finally formulate your research problem. "Reading around" clarifies your purpose, which then suggests a design and makes the choice relatively self-evident.

Hypotheses and questions

Basic differences

Here's the essential difference between the two: a question asks and can receive a definitive answer; a hypothesis, however, can only be substantiated or refuted, never "proven." It is an educated guess—a hunch—that conjectures and then has its credibility tested. Note that the guess is educated, meaning that it's not just some off-the-wall proposition but one that is rooted in knowledge … which means what, in turn? That there's enough studied and written for there to be a body of knowledge in the first place.

So if little is known about your topic (or much is known but not from your particular angle of interest, such as a particular population or setting), chances are it will make good sense to formulate your problem as a question. In that case, you are probably headed toward an exploratory study (see Chapter 10) or perhaps a descriptive study (see Chapter 11). On the other hand, if a great deal is known— enough to formulate an educated hunch about some relationship between variables—then it's likely that a hypothesis may be in order, in which case you are probably headed toward a descriptive study (see Chapter 11), a correlational study (see Chapter 13) or maybe even an experiment (see Chapter 12)!

Commonalities

What hypotheses and questions have in common is that they serve as a framework— your guide for what you'll look at and how you'll look at it. They'll be your concrete reference point for all future action (as in, *What is it I want to know, again?* or *What should I do now?* or *Why should I do that?* or *Why am I reading this article?*) and your standard for analysis (as in, *What am I looking for here, again?* and *What does it all mean?*). The answer is, of course, *Because you're asking X question or testing Y hypothesis.* So remember: whichever you end up with is what you stick to your forehead (figuratively, anyway) to remind you from now on why you're doing whatever you're doing!

The notion of proof

While you're pondering this, remember that we never prove anything in social science; there is just too much fluidity in our subjects of interest. Of course, as noted earlier, questions might be answered definitely; but hypotheses are only substantiated or refuted. Even if it makes sense, then, to articulate your problem as a hypothesis, forget your preconceived notions about proof! Instead, think credible substantiation—particularly within the study's context—and keep your implications for other contexts humble (i.e., conservative).

The null what?

If you do work from a hypothesis, you'll test it with one of several possible tests of statistical significance (see Chapter 24); and what that test will do, in effect, is test the null version of your hypothesis (i.e., your null hypothesis). What in the world is that?

Here are a few examples:

If your hypothesis is: Alcoholism and homelessness are related,

your null hypothesis is:	No siree, they are *not* related.
If your hypothesis is:	Smoking causes lung cancer,
your null hypothesis is:	No siree, smoking does *not* cause lung cancer.
If your hypothesis is:	Race influences social workers' attitudes toward their clients,
your null hypothesis is:	No siree, race does *not* influence their attitudes toward their clients.
If your hypothesis is:	This ten-week special program will change teenagers' behavior,
your null hypothesis is:	No siree, it will *not* change their behavior.
If your hypothesis is:	There is a positive correlation between homelessness and alcoholism,
your null hypothesis is:	No siree, there's *no* correlation between these two variables.

(Of course, the "no sirees" are not a formal part of a null hypothesis! They're just here to make a point.)

Note that a null hypothesis is not an opposite version of your original one; it simply nullifies your proposition, whatever it is.

Why, oh why, such an animal? Well, inherent in the formation of every null hypothesis is the following challenge to the researcher by our nemesis, Mr. Probability Theory, a so-called devil's advocate, who says this: *Guess what? Any differences or associations you find when you test this hypothesis are really just due to chance or sampling error; so don't get too excited!*

Why, oh why, such convolution? Simple, really. Here's the theory. It's so easy to substantiate a beloved hypothesis (yes, even using stats or so-called hard numbers to do so!) that scientific protocol builds into its methodology the requirement that you do all you can to refute it (by doing all you can to substantiate its null version). Then, if your original version still "holds water," your credibility is that much stronger. After all, you can say, *I did everything I could to refute my own proposition, and guess what? It's still a good one!* Just another way of trying to keep research honest. Not such a bad idea.

Is question-driven research real research?

Some people claim that the only *real* research is hypothesis-driven research and that question-driven studies are only precursors to the *real* thing. That's not true and especially not in social science research, which still has much to learn. Each type of study has value and makes sense under certain circumstances; neither one is subservient to the other. And don't let anyone tell you otherwise.

Major points to remember

- There is a logical relationship between the existing state of knowledge about your topic and how you finally formulate a problem for study.
- The literature directs your overall purpose, which logically suggests a design type, which suggests your best means to an end.
- Questions can be asked and answered.
- Hypotheses are educated hunches that conjecture and are substantiated or refuted.
- A null hypothesis argues that the original hypothesis is erroneous and that whatever difference or association it proposes is accidental, not real/true/accurate.
- What hypotheses and questions have in common is that they serve as your concrete reference point for all future action, including analysis.

Exercises

Challenge yourself

1   Develop a question to study in your area of interest. Now from that question develop a proposition to test.
2   Then, challenge yourself. Just how educated is that hunch? From where did you get enough knowledge to make such a hunch?
3   Could you defend that proposition? Could you point to a body of knowledge to support it? If so, then developing a hypothesis-driven study may be legitimate. But if you feel shaky, you might review the literature again to see if you can strengthen your case—or you need to back up and work from a question.

Exercise your null hypothesis

Take a few minutes to practice formulating null hypotheses. Write down five hypotheses and, for each one, formulate its null version. Remember, it's not the opposite of an original hypothesis; it simply states that whatever a hypothesis proposes isn't so.

7

VARIABLES

(A fancy term for a simple idea, that's all)

Key concepts

attribute
conceptual definition
dependent variable
independent variable
level of measure
measurement
operationalization
variation

Introduction

Variables are simply factors that become an object of examination. If variation in age is of interest, then it's a variable. Is gender of interest? Education? Number of siblings? Diagnosis? Work setting? Ethnicity? Religion? Work history? Language? Anxiety? Age? Height? Whatever factors have capacity for variation can be conceptualized and studied as variables.

Defining variables

Research defines variables in two ways: conceptually (the actual concept itself) and operationally (indicators that tell us when we're seeing that variable in action) or in "operation." For some concepts, such as education or even religious affiliation, developing an operational definition isn't difficult. But for complex concepts (constructs) we have some choices about where to start (the conceptual definition) as well as where to end (operational definition). For example, human development has been conceptualized and thus theorized in many ways, from physical to psychosexual to psychosocial to moral to cognitive to gender, to name but a few theoretical viewpoints. For constructs, then, you start by choosing which theoretical paradigm to use for the purposes of your study; and from there you develop the operational definition from that paradigm.

Say you choose a conceptual definition of aggression based on a certain social theory; its operational definition will then consist of the indicators (concrete and observable behaviors) used by that theory to talk about nature and degrees of aggression. In social work research many constructs are of interest; and the challenge is to develop operational definitions that are neither overly simplistic nor reckless. There was a time when ear shape was considered a valid indicator of intelligence, for example. Consider the following:

> *Male social workers publish more than female social workers.*

What do you mean, exactly, by "publish?" What is your operational definition? How will you know it when you see it (its indicators)? Sound like a stupid question? Not really. You might mean professional work only. Or you might want to include any and every kind of publishing, such as popular work outside the profession as well. So be specific.

> *Do you trust your therapist?*
> *X therapy is an effective treatment tool for autistic children.*
> *Are you satisfied with this program?*
> *Religion has an impact in shaping family life.*

What do you mean, exactly, by *trust*, by *effective treatment tool*, by *satisfied*, by *religion*? How are you operationalizing each one? What are their indicators?

Begin by "picking out" the most important variables of your research question as it's phrased and for each, ask yourself:

1 *What do I mean, exactly, by this variable?*
2 *In what way do I want to think about/study (measure) this variable?*
3 *How precise can I or do I want or need to get with this variable?*

In studies that standardize the data collection instrument, operational definitions are necessary precisely in order to pre-fix the questions—to make them specific, closed-ended, clear, and capable of capturing a full range of possible variation. Exploratory studies that seek to identify the important variables obviously can't define the terms as precisely; still, becoming as focused as you can about the object of your interest is useful to either study process. Imagine asking someone your research question or stating your hypothesis and he or she asking for every term in that statement, *What do you mean, exactly?* How would you respond?

Dependent/independent variables

An independent variable is something that you manipulate in a cause-and-effect experiment in order to examine its impact. It's also referred to as X or the "cause." You impose it or offer it in order to test its effect. It might be a special treatment or service, a particular experience, or the use of a certain drug, etc.

A dependent variable, traditionally referred to as Y or the "effect," varies as a result of X, whatever that is; and it is that variation you wish to study. You might be interested in studying variation in skill as a result of the special treatment or service, variation in attitude or knowledge as a result of the particular experience, or change in medical condition as a result of using the drug, etc.

Here's a little tricky something to keep in mind when you are thinking about variables in this way. (In exploratory designs, you do not think in terms of dependent or independent variables; you're just exploring an area of interest to see if you can identify any variables to begin with.) Variables are not inherently independent or dependent. What one researcher might choose to conceptualize as an independent variable—X—(say, level of depression) and conceptualize as a dependent variable—Y—(say, excessive use of alcohol) might be conceptualized in the complete reverse by another researcher. From his or her review of the pertinent literature, Researcher 1 might have concluded that there seems to be a correlation between depression and excessive use of alcohol (from reports, let's say) and decide to formulate this hypothesis:

Depression causes excessive use of alcohol.

In this case, the researcher has—and wishes to test—a hunch that depression causes an excessive use of alcohol. However, another researcher might, from his or her review of the pertinent literature, have noticed the same correlation but has the hunch that excessive use of alcohol can lead to depression. Researcher 2 might, then, formulate the following hypothesis:

Excessive use of alcohol causes depression.

Do you see how in one case one variable (factor) might be seen to have an impact on another while in another case, that very same variable might be seen as the outcome (effect) rather than cause? What's important here is that there be logic in the formulation (see the section on co-variance and causation in Chapter 13)—once again leading you to read enough of the related literature to be "intelligent" in your formulation. (All research roads lead back to a solid review of all possible related literature.)

Measuring variables

While this discussion usually goes into the analysis section of research textbooks, there's something to be said for learning about it earlier than that, for getting a grasp on it as you think about the variables contained in your study and as you think about the instrument you will use to carry it out.

In quantitative studies that require statistics, variables are also said to be measured at one or other level (referred to as LOM, for level of measure). Some can only be measured at a certain level; others can be measured at any one of four possible levels. In effect, to measure a variable is to break it down into the ways you want to look at it in order to study its variation. Sometimes that breakdown is self-evident. For example, eye color can be only measured (broken down) by category of color. But, as noted above, education might be broken down (measured) in various ways. One study might ask if participants completed college. One might ask if they have any college education at all. One might ask about type of school, such as public or private. One might ask respondents to rate the quality of their education compared to that of their peers. And one might ask about number of years of education. And on and on. How a variable is measured (broken down), then, depends on the nature and quantity of information about it that's needed by the study.

Nominal

When you measure (break down) a variable in terms of categories you're said to be measuring it at the nominal LOM. A breakdown of Christian, Muslim, Jewish, and "other" categories for religion, for example, or Democrat, Republican, independent, and "other" for political affiliation reflects nominal LOM. A breakdown of response options such as yes/no, favor/oppose, and agree/disagree also reflects this LOM. Thus, some can only be measured at this level; some we choose to measure this way.

Ordinal

The ordinal level measures (breaks down) a variable not by category but in terms of degrees of difference, rank ordering attributes (variation) from low to high (socioeconomic status, for example) or least to most (as in not at all, somewhat, and very). Rating scales are ways of measuring variables at the ordinal LOM. Numbers are used to reflect degree of difference but only conceptually; they can't be used with any precision. For instance, on a rating scale of 1 to 5 you can't logically say that whoever circled 4 is twice as satisfied with your program as whoever circled 2, only that the person must be quite a bit (an imprecise quantity) more satisfied. You can't say that whoever checked off the "very useful" response option is X times as pleased as whoever checked off the "somewhat useful" option.

Interval

When a variable doesn't have inherent numerical properties (age does, intelligence does not; height does, self-esteem does not), but we choose to break it down and express it in quantitative terms anyway (by "scoring" someone's relationship to that variable, such as degree of self-esteem), we're measuring it at the interval level. Many variables of interest to social science in general and social work in particular are of this type; and using numbers (such as scores) to study them can help us understand their influence.

Major standardized tests, such as IQ, aptitude, college entrance, and many others that score people on such variables as self-esteem, satisfaction, intelligence, depression, aptitude, etc., use this LOM. Here, the numbers used mean more than those used in a rating scale because intervals between 1 and 2 or 60 and 61 are exactly alike. However, the variables are not inherently numerical; we simply use numbers once again to try to understand them, but those numbers have no true zero point. Consider four scores on a test for depression:

Client 1 scores 80 on a test for depression (high)
Client 2 scores 75
Client 3 scores 50
Client 4 scores 20 (low)

Yes, Client 1 scored four times as high as Client 4, who scored two-fifths as high as Client 3. But you cannot say that Client 1 is four times as depressed as Client 4. People are not "four times as depressed" as other people. It's not logical to speak about depression in this way.

In another example, Mr. X scores 700 on a test of bigotry (high) and Ms. Y scores 100 (low). Yes, Mr. X is much more bigoted than Ms. Y, but he's not seven times more bigoted. It doesn't make sense to speak about bigotry in this way. We can only say that he scored seven times as high, indicating a much higher degree of bigotry.

So, we use the interval LOM to quantify the study of a variable that is not in and of itself numerical but we simply choose to treat it as if it were.

Finally, an outdoor temperature of 80 degrees is not four times warmer than 20 degrees; only the numerical interval is four times greater. So, yes, 80 is much warmer than 20, but it's not four times warmer. People often talk this way? Yes. But it's just a way of talking.

Ratio

When we measure (break down) an inherently numerical variable in terms of numbers, we're measuring it at the ratio LOM. Thus, to break down such variables as income, age, height, number of home visits, years in practice or of education, number of clients, birth rate, etc., into their numerical properties is to measure them at this LOM. Because the variable itself is numerical in nature, the numbers used to break it down are also real with a true zero point. Whoever is 66 inches tall *is* twice as tall as whoever is 33 inches tall; at 200 pounds someone *is* twice as heavy as someone at 100 pounds; a caseload of fifty clients *is* five times as large as one of ten.

The ratio LOM is considered the most "sophisticated" level of measurement (way of observing something), because when the time comes for statistical testing to examine the significance of quantitative results, using numbers with real meaning permits the most powerful statistical tests (see Chapter 24).

Major points to remember

- Variables are factors that you decide to make the object of study.
- Variables are defined at two levels: conceptual and operational.
- Operational definitions help us "see" the variable in action (in "operation").
- A major challenge of giving operational definitions to complex concepts is to keep those definitions valid.
- Variables are measured at four levels: nominal, ordinal, interval, and ratio.
- Sometimes the level at which we should measure a variable is self-evident; sometimes we can choose; and the level selected reflects the nature and quantity of information desired by the study about that variable.

Exercises

Self-Test 1

1   Use a few sentences to write down your research topic in general terms.
2   Look it over and, in specific terms, develop a hypothesis or question.
3   Circle the factor/s in that hypothesis or question that you are choosing to study. They are your variables.
4   How will you operationalize them? (How will you "know" them when you "see" them?) Be specific. If for any one someone could ask what you mean by it, it's not specific enough.

Self-Test 2

Ask yourself: *Just how focused do I need to get in order to get the information to answer my research question?*

Self-Test 3

1   For each of the variables you identify above, develop a question or item you might put on a questionnaire along with response options. For each one, identify its LOM. Are you asking for categorical responses? Are you asking for

degree of difference? Would it make sense to give each response a score, such as multiple choice with first response getting 1 point, second getting 2 points, third getting 3 points, etc.? In short, are you asking about something that has real numerical meaning?

2   Provide a rationale for measuring each variable at that particular LOM.

8

ASSUMPTIONS

(Take note! They can make an ass of u and me)

Key concepts

beliefs
knowledge
opinions
proposition
research

Introduction

Like hypotheses, assumptions are propositions, but, rather than test them, you decide to take them as givens for your study. Your hypothesis is a proposition to be studied; your assumptions are propositions to take for granted.

Do all studies make assumptions? Pretty much. Assumptions put studies into context, helping others to understand your mindset as you begin—where you're "coming from." Consider the following hypothesis:

> MSWs with professional education in the social group work method are more likely to catalyze mutual-aid dynamics in their group work practice than MSWs without that education.

The basic assumption in this study is that education has an impact on practice. This assumption is rooted in the research into and knowledge about the impact of education on human behavior (gleaned from reviewing/knowing the literature). Now consider this question:

How do practitioners incorporate grief work into their practice with recovering alcoholics?

The assumption here? That some practitioners do, in fact, incorporate grief work into their treatment; so the problem in this study is how they do it. Here, the researcher will select a sample of persons able to describe how grief work is incorporated into their treatment (who might be practitioners who use grief work or clients who have been in treatment that includes grief work, for example). Excluded from the sample will be practitioners who do *not* incorporate grief work into their practice with recovering alcoholics. You can see that if the question was stated as, *Do practitioners incorporate grief work into their practice with recovering alcoholics?*, the sample would be composed of practitioners who work with recovering alcoholics (to find out if they do/do not incorporate grief work). This question, *Do practitioners incorporate grief work into their practice with recovering alcoholics?*, makes no assumptions about the inclusion of grief work. Instead, it wonders if grief work is even incorporated into treatment. Thus, it is a kind of "backing up" from the previous question. This researcher, then, might select a sample of practitioners who work with persons in recovery and ask them if (not how) they incorporate grief work into their practice. The distinction between the two? If the literature indicates that some practitioners do include grief work in this type of treatment, then it's safe to ask how they do so. However, if it doesn't, then the "if they do" question needs to be asked first.

Types of assumptions

There are basically four types of assumptions, some of which, as you'll quickly see, are safer (more acceptable) to make than others:

From previous research	} formed by reviewing
From knowledge of the subject	the literature
From belief systems	} formed by psychosociocultural
From opinions	life experience

Clearly, the assumptions that carry the greatest weight (thus least likely to be challenged) are those rooted in research and knowledge.

It is important to ask yourself, then, as your problem formulation begins to take shape, *What, if anything, am I taking for granted as I begin this study?* Are you asking a "how" question when perhaps the current state of our knowledge (which you have gleaned from reviewing the literature) in the topic area suggests that you should ask an "if" question at this point? And think about how reasonable your assumptions are; what may seem so to you (as in, all people value social services) may not seem so to others; and strong enough criticism of your assumptions can discredit your entire study.

Major points to remember

- Like a hypothesis, an assumption is a proposition, but one to be taken as a given rather than tested.
- Assumptions need to be acknowledged and specified at the beginning of a study.
- Assumptions come from one of four sources: research, knowledge, belief systems, and opinions.
- Assumptions help to put a study into context.
- Strong enough criticism of assumptions can disavow an entire study.

Exercise

Test yourself

1 Review your research topic.
2 Write down your question or hypothesis.
3 Identify the assumptions that are inherent in it.
4 Talk to others who are knowledgeable about the subject. Do they think your assumptions are reasonable? Why? Why not?
5 Review your question or hypothesis again and change what needs to be changed in order to keep assumptions reasonable. This may mean, like the example above, that you need to "back up" into a more basic question or hypothesis.

9

DESIGN OPTIONS

(So, what's the overall strategy?)

Key concepts

accountability
asking questions
association
correlation
description
design as strategy
examining relationships
experimentation
exploration
hypothesis testing
mixed-method studies
purpose
respondents
subjects
variables

Introduction

Design is a strategy for implementing your study, your guide for all you do from now on. In a nutshell, the function of design is to provide you with guidelines for answering your research question with the least amount of effort, time, and money.

From purpose to design

There are four basic purposes for research, each of which logically leads to a particular design type. As you formulate a problem and think about its importance, then, some kind of logical design framework is probably already beginning to choose you, whether you know it or not!

Purpose 1: Is anything going on here?

This question calls for exploratory design. Its overarching purpose is to gain familiarity with a new or as yet unexplored phenomenon or to achieve new insights into one with which there's already some familiarity but not from the angle you have in mind. We may know a lot about alcoholism in some groups but not among the elderly, for example. It's conceivable, then, that a study of alcoholism among the elderly would be exploratory and another similar study of a group about which we know more would require another design.

Purpose 2: What, exactly, is going on here?

With descriptive design the assumption is that we do know something is going on but not what; hence its overarching purpose is to describe what that is, like taking a snapshot. What might you describe? Many things, such as characteristics of an individual or situation (as in a descriptive case example), or group (as in a particular segment of a client population), or process (as in a counseling interaction), or problem (as in components of a community conflict), or environment (such as the physical layout of a factory), or even the characteristics of a relationship.

Purpose 3: Actually, I think X causes Y

The overarching purpose of experimental design is to test a hypothesis (hunch) that something (X) causes something else (Y). In this case, the literature offers you enough knowledge to formulate a cause-and-effect hunch (pretty bold!) and enough control on the entire research process to impose or offer something and test its effect. It is challenging to develop a research study in which causality is the predominant goal, although practice evaluation has made great strides in this, having innovated several design variations that allow the introduction of comparisons and controls throughout a treatment or service protocol (see Chapter 15).

Purpose 4: Well, perhaps X doesn't cause Y, but I think they're associated

The overarching purpose of correlational design is to test association between variables. It's an attempt to approximate real experiments when you can't control the entire process—either you can't realistically or ethically cause something to happen and then test its effect or you can't randomly assign people into an experimental or control group. It's also referred to as *quasi-experimental* design to connote the fact that it uses the same principles as experiments but with less control.

Like experiments, correlational studies always work from a hypothesis; but experiments generally take place in lab settings or highly controlled scenarios, while correlational studies take place in the "real" world, in situations that are not manipulated ahead of time in order to observe effects.

Constructive combinations

Does it seem like more than one fit is possible for the study you have in mind? That's okay. It's common to have exploration in a descriptive study or to have some description in an experiment. What differentiates them is their overarching purpose; and the label comes from where you place the emphasis. It's also common to read about studies with combined labels, as in exploratory-descriptive, which might then use mixed methods, such as a quantitative measure for some dynamic of interest (e.g., depression) along with a qualitative measure for another purpose (e.g., household income).

In fact, many if not most studies can be conceptualized as "mixed method," with one component of the study seeking quantitative information (because seeking the information of interest makes most sense to do in this manner) and another component seeking qualitative information for the same reason; it makes sense to include an essay response option to a question or to add an interview in addition to a written survey or to observe a group in action in addition to asking them to fill out a questionnaire.

Too many possibilities? Not really—connections give direction

The state of current knowledge, derived from reading the literature, helps you reach a purpose for study by revealing which questions have already been answered, which areas need more probing, and from which perspective a deeper look into a particular territory would be most useful. Once you know your purpose, a design type becomes rather obvious, the only occasional fly in the ointment being feasibility. For example, if your study's purpose suggests that a descriptive study that observes school children in class every day over six months would yield the richest data but the real world impinges with time or cost or accessibility issues, etc., then another road to Rome (in this case, design) needs to be taken.

Major points to remember

- Design is a strategy for implementing your study, a guide for all future action.
- Each of the four basic purposes for research logically leads to a particular design type.
- The overarching purpose of exploratory design is to ask if anything is going on.
- The overarching purpose of descriptive design is to ask what, exactly, is going on.

- The overarching purpose of experimental design is to test cause and effect.
- The overarching purpose of correlational design is to test association (co-presence of variables but not causation).
- Design types may have similarities but are differentiated by their overarching purpose. It's also common to combine elements of different designs in a single study. In fact, most studies seek both quantitative and qualitative information ("mixed-method" studies).
- The state of current knowledge logically suggests a purpose for study by indicating which questions have been answered and which need further probing.

Exercise

Try it on for size

1   Develop a research question for your topic of interest that reflects an exploratory design.
2   Develop a question or hypothesis for your topic of interest that is descriptive in nature.
3   Develop a cause-and-effect hypothesis related to your interest area that would take place in a lab setting.
4   Develop a hypothesis that is not cause and effect but that seeks, in the "real world" (i.e., outside a lab setting), to test association of two variables in your interest area.

10

EXPLORATORY DESIGN

(Is anything going on out there?)

Key concepts

case study
exploration
nonrandom sample
reliability
reviewing literature
survey
validity

Introduction

The overarching purpose of exploratory design is to become familiar with a new phenomenon or to gain new insights into it. That is, we don't know much about the topic of interest, either in general or from the particular angle in which we're interested, so we need to "explore" it.

When to use it?

Exploratory studies can stand on their own, such as ethnographic studies, but often also precede further study into the same phenomenon. When you read about the three common approaches to exploring below, you'll understand why immediately.

Where to begin?

Exploratory studies always work from a question, because you don't have enough knowledge to formulate an educated hunch to test. Because they call for much intuitive reasoning and conceptualization, they're often thought of as the most artistic of the four design types. We have little knowledge to build on, so we rely on intuition to choose a direction of research and our ability to conceptualize in order to identify potential variables.

Three common approaches

There are three common ways of conducting exploratory studies; what they all have in common is the emphasis on fleshing out potentially important variables:

1   **Reviewing the literature**: Literature, both professional and popular, and both from within the profession and outside of it, is used to formulate variables, i.e., factors, to study further. Reviewing the literature is a form of research in and of itself; for example, you might wish to carry out content analysis of the social work literature with regard to the profession's view of certain topics (e.g., populations, problem definitions, etc.) over the years. You might also wish to carry out a review of literature that consists of archival records held in special repositories or in organizations or carry out historical research, closely related, but focusing on a historical perspective. Examining and learning about your topic from what others have said and done in that area of interest is, however, always the first step of all research, regardless of design type, because it is the way in which we make ourselves "intelligent" about the topic of interest—the way in which we provide context for our own study.

2   **Surveying relevant people**: Another way to conduct exploration is to get information from people with practical experience in the area of interest, usually by interview. You're looking for current insights and ideas, and you contact people who might be able to provide them. Like a literature review, your aim is to formulate variables as leads for study, only your focus is on the here-and-now rather than on the written word, which can include study of the past as well.

3   **Case study**: Here you carry out an intensive study of some selected examples that either reflect or are related to the problem of interest. You seek out and analyze selected instances of the phenomenon you're exploring that seem relevant. Sigmund Freud's intensive study of a few patients to gain theoretical insights and Carol Stack Sullivan's long-term participant observation of inner-city kinship networks are good examples of this strategy. Sometimes experts and cases are one and the same. For example, asking social work practitioners to talk about their practice makes them both the object of your study (cases) and experts (on their practice).

Overview of method

1   The sample is nonrandom (see Chapter 18) because your goal is access to information, not generalization.

2   Data collection (see Chapter 19) is generally flexible in order to ensure access to information, and it's usually but not always carried out with instruments that seek qualitative (narrative) data.

3   The measurement concepts of reliability and validity (see Chapter 17) speak primarily to methods and are demonstrated through what is referred to as a "thick" description of the entire study process.

4   Analysis consists of content analysis (see Chapter 21), using some model to make meaning of narrative material.

Major points to remember

* The overarching purpose of exploratory design is to become familiar with a new phenomenon or to gain new insights into it.
* Exploratory studies can stand on their own but often also precede further study into the same phenomenon.
* Exploratory studies always work from a question rather than a hypothesis, because you don't have enough knowledge to formulate an educated hunch to be tested.
* What the strategies all have in common is an emphasis on looking for potentially important variables as food for thought.
* Three common exploratory strategies are: review of the literature; interviewing people for current insights and ideas; and case studies.

Exercise

Check closer for fit

Refer back to the exploratory question you developed in the exercise at the end of Chapter 9. Expand on the process of carrying out an exploratory study by using the above three strategies as your guide. For each:

* How would you begin the study process?
* What types of literature might you read, for example?
* Who might be the experts, and where might you find them?
* What kinds of persons might provide case studies?
* How might you gain access to the experts/case studies?

11

DESCRIPTIVE DESIGN

(Taking a snapshot)

Key concepts

description
generalization
inference
random sampling
sample
population

Introduction

A descriptive design portrays characteristics, both static and dynamic, and works from either a question or a hypothesis, depending on the state of current knowledge. The less information you have the less you can formulate a hypothesis (as in, *More men than women …*); hence, the more logical to work from a question (as in, *Do more women than men …?*). Common descriptive subjects are characteristics of a group, of a place, of a situation, and of a process.

Descriptive studies are interested in generalization (making inferences from a small group—i.e., the sample—to the larger group from which the sample was drawn—i.e., its population). Thus, the concepts of measurement and random sampling are important (see Chapters 17 and 18, respectively). Measurement refers to the reliability and validity of the instrument (your measurement) for study; random sampling is a method of selecting cases to study that gives each one an equal chance of being included. Random sampling is important to descriptive study, because it helps to prevent bias in the final sample and thus permits generalization from it to the larger group of interest.

When to use it?

Descriptive design is called for when your overall aim is to describe a phenomenon, as in a physical environment or the number of different types of case records or the amount and nature of postgraduate training of social workers in a particular state or characteristics of a relationship or demographics or types of behaviors, nature of attitudes, level of knowledge, service utilization, etc. Whenever we wish to get a "snapshot" of something of interest, we generally think description.

Descriptive studies sometimes get a bum rap as not very useful or simply boring. In fact, there's a great deal of room and need for descriptive studies in social work, which, in order to be effective, must carry out its mandates based on what's happening "out there," not on beliefs or assumptions we make about what's happening. It's all too easy to think we know (that there are so many more women than men who attend the program, or that we offer X service so much more than Y service, or that the needs of a particular community are this not that, or that people in this group always behave in that way, etc.). In fact, descriptive studies are often referred to as "corrective experiences" precisely because they help us correct our perceptions, which are too often and easily less than accurate, if only because we rarely have the chance to see any picture in toto.

Where to begin?

Descriptive studies can be launched from either a question or a hypothesis. Which you choose depends on how much is known about your subject. If it seems like there is already a great deal known but you wish to know more, then a hypothesis (remember, it's an educated guess or a "hunch" about something) may be in order. Or it may make sense, depending on the information you are seeking, to phrase your formulation as a question. If you're not sure, ask someone in the know.

Overview of method

1   The sample is random (see Chapter 18) because of the overarching purpose of this design type to generalize. Furthermore, the larger the sample the better (the smaller the likelihood of sample error). Generally, a sample of 30 cases is considered the very minimum, but more often than not we are talking in the hundreds of cases. Also, there are special mathematical calculations through which one can, in fact, identify the optimal (or minimal) size sample required to carry out the study one has in mind.

2   Data collection (see Chapter 19) is predetermined and unchangeable, both as to the use of a standardized instrument and the testing process.

3   The measurement concepts of reliability and validity (see Chapter 17) speak to the integrity of the instrument. Reliability refers to its consistent ability to obtain the same data under the same circumstances. Validity refers to its ability to tap into whatever you want to measure and nothing but that.

4 Analysis consists primarily of statistical analysis of quantitative data (see Chapter 22).

Major points to remember

- A descriptive design portrays characteristics and works from either a question or a hypothesis, depending on the state of current knowledge.
- Descriptive studies are interested in generalization, drawing inferences about a large population of interest from a sample.
- Random sampling and measurement are central to descriptive design.
- Descriptive studies can contribute a great deal to our understanding by providing what are often referred to as "corrective experiences."

Exercise

Check closer for fit

Refer back to the descriptive problem you formulated in the exercise at the end of Chapter 9. Use it to formulate a question or hypothesis around the following four possibilities that you believe, if asked about or tested in some way, would advance knowledge in your topic area:

1 a group
2 a place
3 a situation
4 a process.

12

EXPERIMENTAL DESIGN

(This causes that ... I think!)

Key concepts

cause
control
dependent variable
effect
experiment
group difference
independent variable
plausible alternative explanations
post–test
pre–test
random sampling
rival hypotheses
statistical significance

Introduction

The purpose of experimental design is to test a hypothesis regarding some cause-and-effect relationship (a hypothesis of group difference). In contrast to descriptive design, which aims to describe, experimental design seeks to explain.

When to use it?

An experimental design is appropriate when you meet all three of these criteria:

1   When there's a great deal of knowledge about the topic—enough, in fact, to back up an educated guess about causation. That's pretty educated!
2   When you can actually manipulate whatever you believe to be a "cause" (subject people to it or offer it to them) in order to examine its "effect" (as in a treatment method or drug or experience).
3   When you can control who does or doesn't get that "cause" (as in who does/does not get your treatment or who does/does not get a certain drug or does/does not get to participate in a particular experience).

In some ways, this design type is just the opposite of exploratory design, used when you have very little information.

Where to begin?

In this case, you begin by examining (and re-examining) the implications of this design for the purpose of the study you have in mind. Is an experiment the best (most obvious, least expensive, most reasonable, etc.) way to answer your broad research question? Would an experiment be feasible? Would you be able to both identify and develop an experimental group and a control group? Would you be able to manipulate the intervention (independent variable) you have in mind? In other words, would you be able to offer the experimental group something (such as a new service) while withholding that "something" from another (control) group? Would it be ethical to do so? What would be the implications for the experimental group (the group that gets subjected to your independent variable, also referred to as X)? What would be the implications for the control group (the group that does not get X but gets compared to the experimental group at the outset of the study and again at various later points)? These and other such questions about your ability to control the scenario, if you can, are crucial to determining the appropriateness of an experimental design, especially when you are talking about human subjects.

Concepts basic to this design

*   A *cause* (aka X or *independent variable*) occurs both before and independently of anything else. You want to study its effects and can manipulate it in such a way as to impose it on or offer to others to do precisely that. It occurs/exists first, *independently* of anything else.
*   An *effect* (aka Y or *dependent variable*) occurs as a result of a cause. Its variation, or how it looks as a result of your cause, is what you're interested in examining.
*   An *experimental group* is subjected to (or offered) X, whatever it is. Let's say it's a group treatment option for parenting problems.
*   A *control group* (a group that has the same characteristics as the experimental group) is not subjected to (or offered) X (in this case, let's say a group treatment option for parenting problems). Rather, it is subjected to another type of

intervention (for example, reading material on parenting) or to nothing at all; it just gets "left alone" during the experiment, until your post-test (measure of both groups as the last step of the experiment).

Why use a control group? Because it helps to protect against the possibility that something other than X caused Y (called *plausible alternative* or *rival explanations*; see Chapter 14). In this design, you need to pay attention to external validity (see Chapter 17). Here's how you protect the integrity of the experiment.

Let's say that a group of people with a particular/desirable profile is invited to participate in an experiment. Using a randomization protocol, half of them are assigned into either the experimental or control group. The experimental group gets your X, whatever it is; the control group doesn't (it gets nothing or something else or a placebo). If at the end of the experiment (the end of your X) the two groups differ on what you're testing (say, skill level, which would be called your dependent variable, or Y, and for which you tested both groups at the outset) more than probability theory (chance) would suggest, you can substantiate your hypothesis. If not, you can't.

How do you know that such and such (vagaries of life, passage of time, some public event) *wasn't the reason your experimental group did better on skill?*, asks a challenger. *Well, whatever the experimental group experienced in the world during the program the control group also experienced, and the difference is still significant (so says the results of our statistical testing); so we can rule that possibility out.* That is, if the differences between the two groups at post-test are significant (as revealed by statistical testing), then you can say that they're real/true/accurate, not just an artifact of chance or some unknown factor.

Further, using a randomization protocol to place elements (cases, people, etc.) into either the experimental or control group allows a more unbiased final sample than if you were to pick and choose who/what goes into one group or the other, safeguarding you against sample bias.

TABLE 12.1 The basic experiment: before and after with two groups

	Experimental group	Control group
Pre-tested?★	Yes	Yes
Subjected to X	Yes	No
Post-tested?★	Yes	Yes

★ Using the same measurement tool, the two groups are assessed through statistical analysis for similarities and differences.

Overview of method

1   Randomization (see Chapter 18), a protocol for letting probability theory assign cases into two or more groups (without your interference, in other words), is used to assign members into either an experimental or control group.
2   Design must include the introduction of rigorous controls to eliminate all plausible alternative (rival) explanations (see Chapter 14). These are possible reasons why the outcome of your experiment is what it is—other than your intervention (independent variable, aka X).
3   Data collection (see Chapter 19) is predetermined and unchangeable, both as to the use of a standardized instrument and the testing process.
4   The measurement concepts of reliability and validity (see Chapter 17) speak to the integrity of the instrument you use for measuring the issue of interest. Reliability refers to its consistent ability to obtain the same data under the very same circumstances. Validity refers to the ability of your measurement instrument to truly tap into whatever you want to measure and nothing but that.
5   Analysis consists primarily of analyzing descriptive and inferential statistics (see Chapters 22–24).

Three criteria to show causation

1   X and Y must fit together (co-vary).
2   X (cause) must be able to precede Y (effect); logical, yes?
3   You're satisfied that there are no other plausible (rival) explanations for what you find (see Chapter 14).

Consider the following hypothesis: *Smoking (X) causes lung cancer (Y)*. To claim causality you must show that you always need X (smoking) for Y (lung cancer) to occur and that X (smoking) is sufficient for Y (lung cancer) to occur. So, to substantiate this hypothesis we need to find that smoking is both necessary and sufficient for lung cancer to occur. Today, it's commonly agreed that smoking is enough to cause lung cancer, but there's still some disagreement as to whether it's necessary for lung cancer to occur, since nonsmokers are known to get lung cancer.

Finally, remember that hypotheses are only substantiated, never proven, and so, in reality, we can never completely rule out the possibility that some factor other than X caused Y. Thus, even if we can show causation, it's always tentative and subject to later revision—only viable until later evidence suggests something different. In fact, this kind of design is often used to do just that—to refute "old" theories in favor of new ones.

Major points to remember

- The purpose of experimental design is to test a hypothesis regarding cause and effect.
- An experimental design is appropriate when there's a great deal of knowledge about the topic, when you can formulate a hypothesis and manipulate whatever you believe to be a cause to examine its effect, and when you can control who does/does not get subjected to that cause.
- A cause refers to something that you can manipulate in such a way as to impose it on or offer to others.
- An effect occurs as a result of a cause; its variation is what you examine.
- An experimental group is subjected to or offered the cause. A control group is not subjected to or offered the cause.
- Using a control group helps to protect against plausible alternative explanations.
- If at the end of the experiment the two groups differ on the effect more than probability theory would dictate, you can substantiate your hypothesis.
- Using randomization to assign subjects (cases) into one of the two groups protects against sample bias and allows sample error estimation.
- The basic experiment form includes pre-test, manipulation of X for the experimental but not the control group, and post-test.
- Three criteria for showing causation are that cause and effect must co-vary, that cause precedes effect, and that there are no other plausible alternative explanations for post-test differences.
- To claim causality the cause must be both necessary and sufficient for the effect to occur.

Exercise

Check closer for fit

Imagine the opportunity to carry out an experiment in your area of interest, and formulate a cause-and-effect hypothesis:

- How would such an experiment look?
- Would it be realistic?
- Would it be feasible?
- What might be some obstacles to implementation, and how might you overcome them?

13

CORRELATIONAL DESIGN

(Actually, I don't know if this causes that, but they sure seem to "go" together)

Key concepts

association
control
correlation
ex post facto
hypothesis of association
longitudinal
plausible alternative explanations
quasi-experimental
relational

Introduction

The overarching purpose of correlational studies is to test association; they're "real-world" attempts to approximate true experiments when we don't have control over X—when we can't realistically or ethically cause something to happen in order to test the results. These studies are always framed around a hypothesis.

A correlational study might examine association between variables in one group, such as body image and ethnicity in a group of young adult women (cross-sectional). It might examine association between two groups, such as middle-aged and young-adult women, around a variable of interest, such as body image (comparison). Or it might examine the impact of time on some variable, such as the long-term impact of an eight-week group treatment on attitude and behavior (longitudinal).

An *explanatory* design is used to explore the degree to which two or more variables co-vary—that is, when changes in one variable are reflected in changes in the other variable. A *prediction* design is used to predict certain outcomes in one variable (criterion variable, or anticipated outcome) from another variable (predictor variable). Scatterplots are typically used to graph the form/nature of the association (relationship) between variables in a correlational study, depicting:

- type of association
- existence/nature of extreme scores
- direction of the association (positive or negative)
- degree of the association (weak to strong).

When to use it?

Many relationships can only be studied this way. We can't cause someone to become alcoholic or depressed in order to study their effect, but current knowledge suggests some association. So then what? So we find a way to study the experiences of people who fit the profile of interest—people who are alcoholic or depressed or victims of a natural disaster or children of divorce, etc. And if we find the presence of depression in alcoholic persons, we don't say *alcoholism causes depression* but *Isn't it interesting that when one is present the other seems to be too*? Thus, we carry out a study not with an aim of establishing cause and effect but the strength and intensity of a relationship; ultimately, we might even infer some possible explanations depending on the weight of the results.

Correlational studies are also referred to as *quasi-experimental* to connote the fact that they try to use the same principles as experiments but with admittedly less control.

Where to begin?

If you are interested in the possibility of a relationship between or among factors of interest—that is, an association between or among variables—and there is a significant amount of literature (knowledge) on your subject of interest, *and an experiment makes no sense/is not feasible*, a correlational research design may be in order. Remember, however, that correlational studies do not "prove" a relationship. Rather, they simply indicate that there is some association between or among variables of interest (e.g., depression and excessive use of alcohol), and they can indicate whether an association is positive or negative (related to co-variance or lack thereof between or among variables) and weak or strong. Interest/impetus might come from empirical observation (observing phenomena or dynamics from your practice setting, for example) or from reading reports of research that suggest further study in this form (such as a descriptive study, for example, that identifies the apparent co-presence of certain variables).

Nature of correlation

When association exists and co-variance of variables is in the same direction ("more" of both or "less" of both), correlation is said to be positive. When co-variance exists but takes the variables in opposing directions ("more" of one and "less" of the other), it is said to be negative. Thus, if self-esteem in sixth-grade girls is higher after participating in a special school program, then self-esteem and participation in that program have a positive correlation. If self-esteem is lower, then they have a negative correlation. Both positive and negative correlation can range from very weak to very strong (presented statistically as correlation coefficients). Obviously, the stronger the correlation the stronger the association.

Four common approaches

There are several types of correlational design, and you will find details (utilization, strengths, weaknesses, methods, etc.) in a comprehensive textbook. Here is a brief look at four common designs.

Ex post facto (aka one group post-test only design)

An ex post facto (which means "after the fact") strategy measures (studies) the effect of an event after it has occurred, such as a hostage situation or airplane crash or large-scale blackout or some natural disaster. Clearly, we couldn't cause any one of these things to happen, but their impact is of interest.

Strategy

There is a group (e.g., victims of an earthquake) to be studied?	Yes
There is a pre-test measurement to make?	No
There is an X (e.g., the earthquake) to study?	Yes
There is a 'post-test' measurement (e.g., psychological impact) to make?	Yes

This type of study might be diagrammed as follows: X O

In this case, "X" refers to the variable you wish to study (which has already occurred, hence the inability to do any pre-testing), and O refers to the "post-test" measurement of your group of interest.

Strengths and weaknesses

This strategy allows us to study the effects of phenomena that cannot be studied by experiment. It lacks a control group but occasionally comparison groups may be available; it lacks a pre-test against which the ex post facto measure can be compared (no baseline); and it consists of an accidental sample, which, however, might be random sampled for a final sample to study, making the study more wieldy and allowing generalization from the sample to the larger group … you cannot safely generalize to other groups. Whatever you find out pertains to the sample in question only. Whether or not you can draw some implications from the study— that is another question and depends on the size of sample and the type/s of population for which you might like to examine implications.

Before and after with one group

This design strategy is used when you can pre-test a group before introducing X, whatever it is, such as a group treatment program.

Strategy

There is a group (e.g., adolescent clients) to be studied?	Yes
There is a pre-test measurement (e.g., attitude) to make?	Yes
There is an X (e.g., a ten-week group program) to test?	Yes
There is a post-test measurement (e.g., attitude) to make?	Yes

Strengths and weaknesses

Major strengths are the potential for a pre-test and thus baseline data against which to compare post-test results and control over who gets subjected to X, allowing the possibility of a random sample and reducing the potential for bias. Not having a control or comparison group, however, still leaves you to wonder if it really was X rather than some other unknown factor that caused your results, although the potential for internal validity (see Chapter 14) does increase from the ex post facto design.

Before and after with two groups (aka comparison group pre-test/ post-test design)

This common correlational strategy is used with access to a matching (comparison) group (as in two groups of teens, one of which participates in a ten-week program). Randomizing people/cases into the groups may be possible; if not, you match the groups closely around important characteristics. Then, differences that exist are revealed at pre-test and can be factored into analysis.

TABLE 13.1 Strategy

	Experimental group	Comparison group
Pre-tested?	Yes	Yes
Subjected to X	Yes	No
Post-tested?	Yes	Yes

The formal representation of this design is usually diagrammed as follows:

$$O_1 \qquad X \qquad\qquad O_2$$
$$O_1 \qquad\qquad\qquad O_2$$

In the top line O_1 refers to the pre-test for the experimental group ("observation time 1"), and O_2 refers to the post-test ("observation time 2") for the experimental group. You know this line represents the experimental group, because the "X" between the two signifies the introduction of the independent variable, always represented by the capital letter X. Thus, since you know that this design includes a comparison group, you know that in the bottom line, which has no "X," O_1 refers to the pre-test ("observation time 1") for the comparison group, and O_2 refers to the post-test ("observation time 2") for the comparison group.

Strengths and weaknesses

This strategy most closely approximates a true experiment. Its strengths are the ability to manipulate X (offering a service to some and not to others); the collection of baseline data against which to compare post-test results; and a comparison group to help protect against plausible alternative explanations (see Chapter 14). Thus, here again, the potential for internal validity (see Chapter 14) increases from the previous two designs because of the use of a secondary (control/comparison) group, which if properly selected, will have experienced the same vagaries of the universe that might have confounded the study as the experimental groups, keeping them, all things equal, as similar as they were at the outset of the study except for one's having received an intervention (and thus, hopefully changing as a result of it) and one's having not received it.

Major weaknesses are that randomization of elements into the groups to be compared is not usually possible, and that pre-test results between the experimental and only existing and available comparison group may reveal differences that are too vast to permit any meaningful comparison.

Longitudinal study (aka time series design)

The goal of this strategy is to study the long-term impact, if any, of X. You can study only one group (an experimental group, subjected to X) or, if you have access to a comparison group, two groups. The use of a comparison group helps to reduce the possibility that something other than X explains your findings (see Chapter 23). You might only be able to follow one group, but you might also be able to follow an experimental and a comparison group. Table 13.2 depicts the use of two groups (time series design with comparison group).

In this example the groups are post-tested five times, but you decide how often and how much. If once a year for ten years makes sense to the purpose of your study and is feasible, then do it. If once every three months for two years makes

TABLE 13.2 Strategy

	Experimental group	Comparison group
Pre-tested?	Yes	Yes
Subjected to X	Yes	No
Post-tested time 1?	Yes	Yes
Post-tested time 2?	Yes	Yes
Post-tested time 3?	Yes	Yes
Post-tested time 4?	Yes	Yes
Post-tested time 5?	Yes	Yes

sense and is feasible, then do it. There are no hard and fast rules. Just remember that the longer the study the more difficult it is to follow/find/keep participants. Furthermore, you may be in a position to make observations (take measures of the dependent variable) before the actual introduction of X, in which case the design is referred to as an *interrupted time series design*, which might have the strategy shown in Table 13.3.

TABLE 13.3 Strategy

	Experimental group	Comparison group
Pre-tested time 1?	Yes	Yes
Pre-tested time 2?	Yes	Yes
Pre-tested time 3?	Yes	Yes
Subjected to X	Yes	No
Post-tested time 1?	Yes	Yes
Post-tested time 2?	Yes	Yes
Post-tested time 3?	Yes	Yes

This kind of design, following one group only (i.e., no comparison group), and having taken a series of pre-test measures to develop a stronger baseline than a one-shot pre-test only (in this case, measuring four times), might be diagrammed in this way:

$$O_1 \quad O_2 \quad O_3 \quad O_4 \quad X \quad O_5 \quad O_6 \quad O_7 \quad O_8$$

Here, the first four observation points represent the baseline over some period of time, X represents the intervention (independent variable, e.g., a type of treatment or service), and the second four observation points represent a series of post-test measures.

Strengths and weaknesses

This strategy permits a long-term look at the stability of X. Pre-testing allows a baseline measure against which to make post-test measures. Furthermore, with a comparison group, the potential for plausible alternative explanations (see Chapter 14) decreases—i.e., the potential for internal validity increases. A weakness, which is not inherent in the design but often comes into play anyway with this strategy, is the great potential for sample attrition.

Overview of method

1   You try to introduce some degree of randomization protocol to assign cases into either your single group for study or into two groups, an experimental group and a control or comparison group.
2   Design must include consideration of plausible alternative (rival) explanations (see Chapter 14).
3   Data collection (see Chapter 19) is predetermined and unchangeable, both as to the use of a standardized instrument and the testing process.
4   The measurement concepts of reliability and validity (see Chapter 17) speak to the integrity of the instrument. Reliability refers to its consistent ability to obtain the same data under the same circumstances. Validity refers to its ability to tap into whatever you want to measure and nothing but that.
5   Analysis consists of statistical analysis of quantitative data using the language of correlation coefficients (see Chapters 22–24).

Major points to remember

•   Correlational studies attempt to approximate real experiments when we can't realistically or ethically manipulate X.
•   The overarching purpose of correlational studies is to test association, or how variables relate to each other, both in nature and strength.
•   Correlational studies are often used to study the impact of major natural disasters or other phenomena (such as alcoholism, divorce, mental illness, etc.) that we would not cause in order to study but the results of which are interesting and important to understand.
•   Correlational studies test hypotheses when there is a strong enough knowledge base in the subject to make an educated guess of association.
•   Co-variance of variables can be either positive or negative and can range from very weak to very strong in either direction.
•   As much randomization as possible increases the credibility of this design.
•   Four common approaches are: ex post facto, before and after with one group, before and after with two groups, and longitudinal.

Exercise

Check closer for fit

Refer back to the correlational study you formulated in the exercise at the end of Chapter 9. Use that hypothesis to develop the following:

1 a before-and-after study with one group
2 a before-and after study with one experimental and one comparison group
3 a longitudinal study of one group.

14

PLAUSIBLE ALTERNATIVE EXPLANATIONS

(How do you know it wasn't ...?)

Key concepts

bias
comparison
control
internal validity
rival explanation

Introduction

Other than a mouthful to say, plausible alternative explanations are simply hypothetical rival explanations for your findings. They apply most directly to experimental and correlational designs. How to respond to these rivals? In effect, you try to eliminate them by anticipating them as the study is designed. Most of them are eliminated by using a control group (which means experiments have the best chance of really eliminating them) or with a well-chosen comparison group in correlational studies. To eliminate rival explanations is to increase the potential for internal validity.

How do they fit in?

Say you're interested in tenant attitudes and wonder if an educational program would be effective in changing attitudes toward organizing. You locate a group of tenants and test them on attitudes toward tenant organization with a questionnaire (your pre-test). You then offer them the educational program, and when it ends you administer the same questionnaire (your post-test).

Your results suggest that their attitudes toward organizing are much more positive after the program. Great! You get ready to give a report to a potential future funding source, one that is interested in helping you to organize your community. And just as you're getting ready, along come a couple of killjoys who ask you how you know that the attitude change is really due to your program:

> *How do you know some external events during your study* [such as publicity about tenancy in the newspapers or on television] *didn't cause the change in attitude?* asks one of them. *Well,* you respond, *we used a comparison group. We couldn't use a control group because we didn't carry out this study in a lab; but we did find a similar tenant group, and whatever external events might have occurred would have influenced both groups. Yet, when we post-tested them, there was still a significant difference between them.*
>
> *I see,* he says, *but how do you know your experimental group wasn't in some way unusual and perhaps especially susceptible to change without your program and so was biased to begin with? Because,* you answer, *not only did we choose our groups very carefully but by pre-testing both we saw that they're in fact very comparable. And so again, even if our experimental group was biased, so was the control group, and the differences were still significant between them after the program.*
>
> *Well then,* your interrogator continues, *how do you know that the attitudes of the experimental group didn't change simply because of all your attention? A good point,* you concede, *but one we thought about! We gave both groups attention—not the same kind but attention just the same. So both groups got attention,* you respond with a smug smile.

Now your challengers are becoming rather impressed, so of course they seek to argue further:

> *What about natural maturation?* asks Killjoy #2 rather haughtily. *How do you know that your experimental group didn't change simply because they matured during your program? Well,* you respond self-assuredly, *they probably did, but so did the members of the comparison group, and again, the differences between them after our program were still significant!*

Now the killjoys are really looking to trip you up!

> *How about the fact that you* did *pre-test everyone?* asks Killjoy #1 slyly. *Couldn't just taking the pre-test have gotten your experimental group to thinking and caused the change? Oh, sure,* you quickly agree, *but to eliminate this small possibility, we'd have to have given up the chance to pre-test, and we'd rather acknowledge the small chance that pre-testing may have had this effect. Anyway, if it did affect the experimental group, it also affected the comparison group, and the experimental group still did better at post-test.*

Now Killjoy #2 pipes in again:

> *Well, isn't it possible that just being part of the testing process caused the changes? After all, they took the same test twice. Perhaps the changes are simply due to a practice effect … That's true,* you agree, *but again, we thought this possibility was only slight and so chose the option of having baseline data.*

Looking increasingly impressed by your thoughtfulness, he adds:

> *What if the members of your experimental group tried to please you with certain answers or to outwit you in some way with post-test answers? Yes,* you acknowledge, *that's always possible. So we used slightly different versions of the same questionnaire to help prevent this kind of manipulation.*

Finally, as if dredging up the last challenge, Killjoy #1 wonders if perhaps the standards of analysis at post-test weren't different from those at pre-test (i.e., lower):

> *Perhaps,* he argues, *your observers were more tired, less enthusiastic, less careful at the end of the project than at the beginning. … Or in the converse, perhaps they were more skilled at post-test? Either way, a bias would be introduced, no? Yes,* you agree that these are possible. *However,* you reply, *we trained our researchers carefully and thoroughly.*

Apparently convinced and very impressed by your thoughtfulness (but depressed by their inability to find obvious flaws in your study), the two killjoys prepare to leave. As they approach the door, Killjoy #1 stops and yells:

> *Aha! I just remembered that when looking over your report I noticed that about 25 percent of the experimental group dropped out before the end of the program! What about it?* he asks excitedly. *Maybe those who stayed were biased in some way and that's what caused your findings, not the program itself! Uh oh,* you say, *that's true; it is a real possibility (i.e., plausible alternative explanation for your findings) that we didn't consider.*

After you escort the killjoys out of your office, you ask yourself if you could have made the program shorter so that more people might have stayed. You're not sure. Or could you have done more to convince people how important it was to the study to stay until the end? Probably. Oh well, live and learn …

The plausible alternative (rival) explanations identified in the above scenario are the major ones that you need to attend to; check a comprehensive research textbook to identify others and to learn more about the details of eliminating them. But you get the point. Internal validity is a big deal for experimental and correlational studies.

How big a worry are they?

Well, in effect, plausible alternative (rival) explanations are as big a worry as you want to make them. You should always think about the internal validity of the data produced by your study. However, potential rival hypotheses are always considered at the outset of, and integrated into the methods of, any good experimental or correlational study. It's especially expected that experimental studies, which make the boldest claims (cause and effect), will introduce all rigor possible to reduce their threat; clearly, it's less possible for correlational studies to do as much. The point here is, in a nutshell, that as many factors that might have a significant influence on your findings be considered so that if killjoys appear when you're done and ask, *But could it have been such and such that accounted for the change?* you're well prepared to respond.

Major points to remember

- Plausible alternative explanations are potential rival explanations for your findings. The more you can eliminate them the more legitimate become claims of causality or association.
- Most plausible alternative explanations are eliminated by using a control or comparison group; some are mitigated by using different but equivalent pre-test and post-test instruments; the threat of some is reduced by carefully training researchers and participants.
- The most common plausible alternative explanations are described and discussed in every research textbook.
- All experimental and correlational studies must attempt to eliminate as many rival explanations as possible in order to achieve a high degree of internal validity.

Exercise

Do they apply?

Look back over some of the hypotheses you've formed as practice exercises. For each one:

1   Can you identify some challenges in the form of those identified above that might come your way?
2   What might you do to reduce the threat of plausible alternative explanations in each case? What kind of actions (controls) would you have to take (introduce)? Would they be feasible? Why or why not?
3   Would you have to change/revise the study in any way? How so?

15

PRACTICE EVALUATION

(So, are you doing good stuff or what?)

Key concepts

clinical research
collaboration
effectiveness
experimental single-case study
idiographic study
intra-unit comparison
N = 1
single-subject design
single-system design
time
time series design

Introduction

Practice evaluation (aka clinical research, single-subject or single-system or time series design, N = 1, or idiographic or experimental single-case study) moves the practitioner away from theorizing about the value of what he or she does to giving it a critical look by studying its impact on client systems, which, for this design, might be individuals, dyads, groups, or any entity, in fact, that you conceptualize as a system and for which goals can be expressed and your progress toward those goals can be tracked. If you study the effect of a certain therapy for couple counseling, the couple is your system, and you measure how the couple does as a couple. If you study the impact of certain interventions on group cohesion, the group is your system, and you measure how the group does as a group.

Clearly, some things (such as behavior) are easier to track than others, but the inventory of instruments to measure both complex processes and complex issues grows every day. So in this design the practice (treatment/service) you carry out is X, your independent variable; and its effect (as in changes in mood states or behavior or skill) is Y, your dependent variable.

In contrast to experiments or correlational studies, which make inter-group comparisons, this design is interested in *intra-system* comparison—in comparing a system with itself over time by tracking the impact on it of your intervention. And its ultimate aim is not generalization but replication—to carry out enough similar studies to be able to draw inferences of effectiveness about a piece of practice (treatment/service). Yes, you can already discover some of that by examining its impact on one system; but the more you repeat it with other like systems and get the same results, the stronger your claims of effectiveness can be.

Mindset

The mindset for practice evaluation is *collaboration*. We don't impose practice, and we don't impose practice evaluation. We explain purpose, contract around goals, and request agreement and close collaboration in conceptualizing, developing, implementing, and analyzing process and progress. In fact, that the components of evaluation so closely resemble those of practice make this design very complementary to practice. They are:

Practice evaluation	*Practice*
• Specify the problem to examine (e.g., level of anxiety), which becomes Y, your *dependent* variable.	• Identify and examine the problem/s to be addressed.
• Measure that problem (i.e., nature and frequency of symptoms) with an assessment tool.	• Assess the problem/s in order to shape the course of treatment/service.
• Specify the intervention to evaluate, including a proposed time frame. That becomes X, your *independent* variable.	• Determine which treatment/service to implement, along with some attention to a time frame.
• Assess changes in the nature of the problem over time using the tool used originally.	• Assess, against original needs and goals, client system progress as treatment/service is carried out.

When to use it?

This type of design is best suited to tracking symptoms that can be easily measured or observed. Thus, the more complex the dependent variable (problem to be tracked), the more difficult (or at least complex) it may be to partialize it into components that can be tracked easily and reliably (although, as noted previously, increasingly good instruments are becoming available as social workers become increasingly interested in evaluating their practice methods).

Overview of method

Before treatment/service begins, a measurement tool is selected (either an existing one or one developed specifically for this purpose) and baseline measures (this design's version of a pre-test) of the problem (Y) taken. Three to five measures are ideal, but even two can begin to build a visual pattern. Results are plotted on a graph, giving a picture of where things stand before your intervention (X, sometimes referred to as T in the context of practice evaluation). For example, a couple might track the number of fights each day before they begin their sessions, or you might rate group cohesion at the next meeting before introducing a particular intervention.

Treatment/service (X/T) then begins, regular measurements of the system continue (status of the problem assessed), and the results are plotted on the graph. When and how often? You decide whatever makes sense.

At the end of the intervention, or at least at the end of its research component, you eyeball the graph for one of three possible correlations: positive (the more you intervened the better the system did); negative (the more you intervened the worse it did); or no apparent correlation (your intervention seems to have made no difference), which is arguably as bad an outcome as a negative correlation.

A few variations

AB Design on one variable

In talking about her problems, your client says she can't seem to stop crying. Together you decide to track her crying spells as one way of determining how she's feeling and if your treatment is helping her feel better. She's going to see you three times a week; and she's to keep track of her crying spells on a daily basis. At each visit you'll record the daily number of spells since the last visit on a graph and look it over together (Figure 15.1). Her first visit is scheduled for five days later;

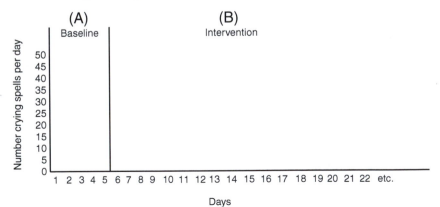

FIGURE 15.1 AB Design on one variable (days 1–5 equal before intervention; 6 equal first day of intervention)

and she's to track her crying spells every day until her first visit as a baseline. That baseline is "A," and your treatment (intervention) is "B."

The AB Design is subject to many possible rival hypotheses (*How do you know it was your intervention that produced the result and nothing but?*), making strong conclusions difficult. Variations, such as those below, begin to introduce some controls against rival hypotheses, permitting stronger conclusions about the effect/s of the intervention.

ABAB Design on one variable

Let's say you go on vacation for two weeks. Rather than end the study, you and your client decide she'll continue to track her progress while you're away (A2) and when you return you'll continue the treatment (B2) and also see how it went for her while you were away (Figure 15.2). This design is also known as *single-subject experiment* because A2 (when you're away) serves as a "case control" by reflecting what happens when X stops for any reason after X/T.

Clearly, the introduction of a case-control period begins to help you control for possible rival hypotheses regarding the effects of your intervention. If regression occurs during your absence (the withdrawal of the intervention), there is a message about the intervention. It is then important to explore and examine that message. Is it true regression in the absence of treatment/service? Did something particular happen in the life of the client system to create a regression? Or, in the alternative, did the client remain stable during the absence of the intervention? If so, what might that signify? Is that a good thing? Do you wish your client regressed when you were away so you could be sure that it is your presence that has the desired treatment/service effect? (Just kidding, of course! Naturally, you would not wish this—at least your professional self would not wish this, but this is all important food for thought about the impact of your intervention.)

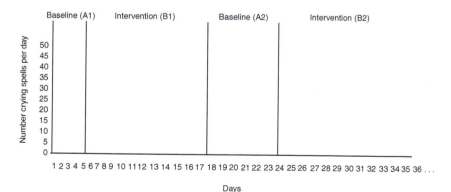

FIGURE 15.2 ABAB Design on one variable (days 1–5 equal before intervention; 6–7 equal original intervention; 18–24 equal case-control period; 25 plus equal renewed original intervention)

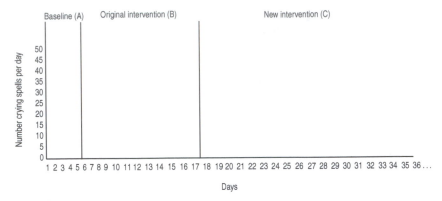

FIGURE 15.3 ABC Design (days 1–5 equal before any intervention; 6–17 equal original intervention; 18+ equal new intervention)

ABC Design

Another scenario: let's say you, your client, or both aren't satisfied with her progress as it regards B, the period during which you implemented your first intervention (weekly talk therapy). You consult with your supervisor and brainstorm another approach that includes certain structured daily homework. Your client agrees, so you replace your weekly talk therapy sessions with this structured homework. Figure 15.3 shows what that graph looks like.

Analysis

First, eyeball your graph at the end of the study period (or at regular intervals if your study is long term) to see if a dramatic enough pattern exists to gauge success. If not (often the case), a simple statistical test can be used to examine if the difference between what would be expected (theoretical probability) and what really happened (reality) is significant.

Choosing the system

One way to guard against (your) biasing the project and a way to introduce some control into this design is to let probability dictate who or what will become your study system. For example, out of all the cases that fit the profile, use a random process to determine which one you'll invite to participate. Or decide that the next new case with the right profile that's presented to you (walks through the door, is referred, etc.) will be the one you invite.

Issues to consider

1   The choice of client system, intervention/treatment (X/T), and problem to address (Y) must be professionally logical and theoretically sound, not just

seem like a good idea at the time. This means you must have "read up" or must "read up" about the problem at hand including past and current approaches, etc.

2   Your goals (changes in Y, the dependent variable) must be reasonable.

3   Consider collecting quantitative or qualitative data (or both) and any feasible collection method.

4   The measurement instrument must be stable (reliable), sensitive (valid), and fairly easy to use.

5   Rating can take place during practice or later.

6   Many sources of information can be considered. Who's the best source? The client system? You? Someone else? If so, who? A colleague? A family member? A teacher? Now consider the study's purpose and the best source given the desired perspective. And now, consider triangulation (more than one source).

7   Have a time frame in mind, and think relatively short term. This design is not intended to be open ended.

8   Think about bias, particularly yours. (You can see the potential for wanting to see progress where it may not exist, yes?)

Major points to remember

- The overarching purpose of single-system design is to measure change over time (i.e., intra-system comparison); thus, time is always an element in this type of study.
- Systems might be individuals or groups or any entity that can be conceptualized as such and for which goals can be expressed and the process can be tracked.
- Practice (treatment/service) is the independent variable (X/T) in this design and its effect (as in changes in mood states or behavior or skill) is the dependent variable (Y).
- The ultimate aim of single-system design is replication, not generalization.
- The components of practice evaluation closely resemble those of practice.
- The mindset for practice evaluation is collaboration, from conceptualization to analysis.
- The methodology consists of selecting a measurement tool, taking baseline measures, introducing an intervention, taking measures during that intervention, and analysis.
- Choices of client system, intervention, and desired outcome must have a logical and theoretical basis.
- All data collection methods can be used; either practitioner or client may act as rater; and rating can take place during actual practice or later.
- To select a source of information, consider the study's purpose and the best source given the perspective desired; and consider triangulation.
- The instrument used must be stable, sensitive, and fairly easy to use.
- The study should be relatively short term.
- Consider the potential for practitioner bias.

- This design is most well suited to tracking symptoms that are easily measured or observed or for which instruments have been specifically constructed and found both reliable and valid.
- The more you can let probability dictate who ends up as your study system of N = 1, the better.

Exercise

Ask yourself

How might this design fit into the work I do?

1   Choose a client system from among your caseload.
2   Identify its general problem.
3   Select a dependent variable (i.e., a symptom of that problem you'd want to change).
4   Select an independent variable (i.e., the treatment/service you'd implement).
5   Select or develop the instrument you'd use to test changes in the dependent variable.
6   Develop a process, including what you would do (exactly) and for how long.
7   Using the graph outline in Figure 15.1, plot a graph that would illustrate success (AB).
8   Now plot a graph that would illustrate stabilization while you're away on vacation (ABAB).
9   And now plot a graph that would illustrate a change in treatment (ABC).

16

PROGRAM EVALUATION

(So just how good are we?)

Key concepts

accountability
assessment
consumer empowerment
documentation
evaluation
monitoring
politics

Introduction

Program evaluation is the study of organizations, many aspects of which are of interest, such as program design, planning, implementation, monitoring, and effectiveness (often referred to as outcome studies). The ultimate goal of program design is professional accountability, which goes hand in hand with consumer empowerment by making visible and even public who's doing what to whom; how, how much, and why; and whether or not what's being done is meeting professional service mandates efficiently, effectively, and ethically (Smith, 2010).

Program evaluation includes questions about planning and design (before, during, or after the fact), such as assessments of needs, goal appropriateness and achievement, design and development structures, the nature of interventions required, and evaluation of achievement.

It also asks questions (before, during, or after the fact) about the quantity and quality of services offered, the nature of their implementation (as in the nature of service providers), projected or real successes and failures, possible design flaws, and costs. And outcome studies examine the impact of what we do—its effectiveness in real-world terms. In other words, are we really helping anyone?

Mindset

Michael Smith (2010) suggests that there are four ways to think about program evaluation:

1   as a research method, which provides a scientifically accepted protocol for selecting a problem to study, selecting a design, obtaining a sample, collecting data, and analyzing results, helping to prevent biased or haphazard judgments;
2   as a form of practice by providing a way of rendering a service to an organization as a client by helping it examine its internal and external needs, health, and welfare;
3   as a field of study, which assesses the quality of our social policies, programs, and interventions and offers special techniques for evaluating efficiency and effectiveness;
4   as a political process, the methodological rigor of which helps to ensure that we're seen as objective investigators in the never-ending political environment of competing needs, values, and ideologies.

Applying design types to program evaluation

Exploration

Professionals related to the services offered by the organization, or literature that provides a history of service in a similar or related area, can be helpful in program design and planning and even for evaluation purposes, such as comparing approaches to service. Interviewing employees with practical experience in a particular area of organizational interest can give you a flavor of the informal system, for example, or of professional and/or interdisciplinary dynamics and of organizational norms, cultures, and subcultures. Many subcultures exist in hospitals, for example, which house many disciplines all trying to collaborate toward common goals. And finally, you might also carry out case studies, such as the intensive study of one department, one client group, or one system of service.

Description

How many times have you believed one thing about an organization only to discover that you were wrong, wrong, wrong? Well, that's what a corrective experience is, and that's what descriptive studies do. There's plenty of room for and value to program-related description of all kinds, ranging from taking snapshots of management to service providers to service consumers and from an organization's internal environment (who's doing what to whom and how) to its external one (the larger context within which the organization operates, including physical, political, and economic climates).

If program evaluation is about professional accountability, then we need to keep track of what we're doing. And if it's about consumer empowerment, then we need to know what we're doing, not operate on assumptions or beliefs.

Experimentation

The purpose of experimental design is to test cause and effect. So, can an experiment be carried out under the rubric of program evaluation? Think about your practice setting. Let's see …

1   Do you have a lot of knowledge about a topic of organizational interest? Enough to formulate a hypothesis? If so, move on.
2   And can you imagine ethically causing something (subjecting people in or related to the organization to it or offering it to them) in order to examine its effect: a special program, a special approach to service, a new policy, a new program, a new service provider, a new intake process, a new discharge process? If so, move on.
3   Can you imagine being able to ethically control who would be subjected to or offered whatever you want to test? Management? Employees? Clients? Related others? If so, move on.
4   Can you imagine obtaining a control group? Ethically using some form of randomization to determine from a single pool who will and who won't get subjected to or offered what you want to test? If so, you may be able to conduct an experiment! If not, move on.

Correlation

If it isn't feasible or ethical to conduct an experiment, maybe you can test for association, or correlation. You might examine association between variables in a client group, for example, such as gender and patterns of attendance, or in an employee group, such as level or type of position and use of the Employee Assistance Program (EAP). Clearly, you can't manipulate patterns of attendance or use of the EAP, but you can try to examine them in relation to other variables for certain groups of interest. Or you might test association between two groups, such as the day shift and the night shift support staff, around a variable of interest, such as absenteeism. Again, you can't force absenteeism in order to study it, but as a supervisor you might be interested in association between shift and absenteeism patterns. And as practitioner, program designer, or fund-raiser you might be interested in the long-term impact of a particular organizational approach to service on a variable such as recidivism rate.

See each of the chapters on these design types for more ideas about how each one might be used for program evaluation.

Logic models

A *logic model* (aka *logical framework*, *theory of change*, or *program matrix*) is a tool used in program evaluation to evaluate effectiveness. It usually consists of a graphic depiction of what is considered to be a logical relationship between the following:

1   *resources* (what and how many resources in a program, e.g., human, financial, etc.);
2   *activities* (what the program actually does, e.g., training);
3   *outputs* (what the program produces as a result of its activities, e.g., practitioners trained in a particular treatment approach);
4   *outcomes* (changes or benefits that occur as a result of that production, e.g., more successful treatment of a particular presenting problem).

Logic models are often used in the evaluation stage of a program, but they might apply to planning or implementation as well. Whichever the case, the central purpose is to assess causal relationships between elements of a program (an "if–then" relationship), the driving logic being as follows:

1   *If* resources are available, *then* activities can take place;
2   *If* activities take place (successfully, of course), *then* desired outputs can be expected; and
3   *If* outputs occur as planned (logically), *then* outcomes (planned/desirable) can be expected as well.

Overview of method

The basic steps of program evaluation according to Smith's (2010) model are:

1   Describe the program to be studied through qualitative or quantitative data or both (program statistics, interviews, questionnaires, etc.). With this you provide a context for implementation.
2   Define program goals (using formal documentation, such as mission statements, by-laws, formal program goals, etc.) to determine differences between what was intended and what is really in fact happening. With this you provide a context for analysis.
3   Select a design:
    (a)   Select an overall design based on your study's purpose.
    (b)   Select a data collection plan: any of the three major methods are appropriate (see Chapter 19).
    (c)   Select a sample—either an entire population or a sample, depending on real numbers. In all but exploratory studies, some form of randomization is used to show that the sample isn't biased (as in selecting people who are most positive about a program).

4   Implement the study (note: with sensitivity to the environment, i.e., agency considerations).
5   Analyze the data (note: with an eye to the politics of the context).
6   Report your results to the organization (in a manner that can be heard/is constructive).

Large-scale descriptive or other studies that collect quantitative data are often of interest to those in policy positions, program planners, and development and fund-raising personnel. Smaller studies or those that focus on collecting qualitative data are often of interest to program planners and practitioners. But remember, they're all being delivered in a political climate; so be rigorous in method, be sensitive in implementation, and be aware in reporting. What you find may be difficult for agency representatives to hear. Find ways to say what you have to say (use your practice skills to frame your findings in such a way that they can be integrated into program planning).

Major points to remember

*   Program evaluation is the study of organizations with goals of professional accountability and consumer empowerment.
*   Conceptualized as a research method, program evaluation provides a scientifically accepted protocol for the study process and helps to prevent biased or haphazard judgments (Smith, 2010).
*   Conceptualized as practice, program evaluation provides a service by helping an organization examine its internal and external health (Smith, 2010).
*   As a field of study, program evaluation assesses the quality of social policies, programs, and interventions (Smith, 2010).
*   Because program evaluation is always carried out in a political environment, its rigor helps to ensure that the investigator is and is seen as objective (Smith, 2010).
*   All major designs (exploratory, descriptive, experimental, and correlational) can be considered.
*   Any of the three major methods of data collection or combination thereof can be considered.
*   In all but exploratory studies, random sampling is used.
*   Analysis consists of whichever type is appropriate to the data collection method used.
*   A logic model is a program evaluation tool that assesses causal relationships between elements of a program (resources, activities, outputs, and outcomes).

Exercise

Try it on for size

Think about the many types of organizations, public and private, that exist in relation to your topic of interest.

1   Now, applying each of the four major types of design as outlined above, how might you carry out a piece of program evaluation in one of those organizations?
2   What internal and/or external and human or other resources would you need to carry out the study?
3   What obstacles might you encounter? Could any of them be overcome? How so?
4   How might each of the four design types be applied to study of the internal working of the organization?
5   How might they be applied to a study of the organization's service delivery mechanisms?
6   In each case, how would you go about developing a sample? Would you use any form of randomization or random selection or not? In either case, why or why not, and what difference would it make?
7   What kinds of data collection instruments might be appropriate?
8   Who, both inside and outside of the organization, might be interested in your findings?

Reference

Smith, M. (2010). *Program Evaluation in the Health and Human Services.* New York: Springer Publishing Company.

17

WORKING TOWARD RELIABILITY AND VALIDITY

(Is your ruler correct? And are you getting to the heart of the matter?)

Key concepts

accuracy
asking the right questions
clarity
consistency
integrity
knowing "it" when you see "it"
measurement
observation
operationalization
reliability
specificity
validity (external)

Introduction

The concept of measurement is central to instrument design; and to talk about measurement is to talk about reliability and validity. How they pertain in particular to qualitative data is discussed more specifically in Chapter 21.

Reliability in brief

Reliability is when you use an instrument with a group of people, turn the clock back, use it again with them in exactly the same conditions, and get exactly the same results. A rubber ruler, for example, is not as reliable as a metal ruler. In the case of a research instrument, you are concerned with extreme clarity (in instructions, in item construction, etc.) and with extreme attention to the formulation of items (e.g., that each item in the instrument is stated in a manner that leaves no room for ambiguity on the part of the respondent). You are also concerned with reliability among raters (should, for example, you hire a few observers to observe behavior in a group). Here too your directions are crystal clear, and each "observer" (rater) knows exactly what to rate how and why. In other words, one observer might not rate one group member as inactive while another would conclude that even though this member did not speak during the observation he or she was very active with eye movement, body language, etc. Both raters would have received clear instructions about what constitutes "activity."

Validity in brief

Validity is when an instrument taps into (measures) what you want to tap into and nothing but that. Thus, a metal metric ruler may be reliable (because it's not going to change shape according, for example, to heat or cold, which might in fact affect a rubber ruler), but it's not a valid measure of inches. Only a ruler that measures inches is a valid tool to measure inches; this is a pretty self-evident concept. It becomes a bit more complex, however, in talking about research. There are different types of validity that one strives for, some related specifically to the purpose of the research, and some more solid than others (more below).

Let's say you want clients' opinions about your agency service. You might ask, *Has X service been useful to you?* (with yes/no options) or *How do you feel about X service?* (with response options ranging from "very good" to "very poor"). But if you want to know what they think (opinion), you need to ask exactly that. Asking about utility isn't exactly like asking for opinion. And asking for feelings doesn't reach for opinions either. Picky picky picky? Yes, but for a good reason. Only asking for exactly what you want makes your question (item) valid.

Clearly, for a whole instrument to be reliable and valid, each item on it has to be designed with those goals in mind as well. Thus, this discussion pertains to those two levels, and when you think about these concepts, think of the whole instrument and of each item on it as well.

Let's say you're interested in anger in children. You train ten people to observe children at various school playgrounds, all to use the same checklist with concrete indicators of anger "in action" (operation). What will that checklist contain? How will observers "know" anger when they see it? Clearly, those behaviors that are easiest to note clearly by all of the raters (like seeing someone hit someone or sticking out a tongue, foot stomping, or crying) are the most reliable. But are they all valid indicators of anger *and nothing but anger*? Of course not. You can probably come up with a couple of reasons other than anger for each of these behaviors. Designing items that are both reliable and valid is not always easy, then; and instruments intended to measure complex phenomena can often be a long-term (pre)occupation—field tested over and over again and subjected to review, content analysis, and statistical tests for reliability and constantly compared and contrasted with the existing (updated) literature for validity.

A balancing act: purpose and trade-offs

Two good rules of thumb to follow:

1   The clearer and more specific the questions and the fewer the response options, the higher the potential for reliability. Thus, a yes/no response option is very reliable. It's highly doubtful that if you answer *yes* once (let's say, to a question about whether you like chocolate) and turn the clock back *to the very same circumstances* you'd then answer *no* to that same question. If I love chocolate on Tuesday, and I wake up on what I think is Wednesday to find that it is in fact Tuesday again, I am more than likely to (still/again) love chocolate.

2   On the other hand, the more the questions capture the range of possibility in response options (the full flavor of possibilities), the higher the potential for validity. Thus, while a yes/no response option is highly reliable, response options like "very much in favor," "in favor," "somewhat in favor," "neutral," "somewhat against," "against," and "very much against" are more likely to capture subtleties or the gray areas, where many people fit on many issues. Some people might feel very strongly about an issue and thus, *very much in favor* captures their feelings, while some might feel in favor but would not necessarily say *very much in favor*.

Since these two rules seem to contradict one another, can you achieve both? You can certainly work toward both and achieve a high level of each. Instruments are often tested for years to do just that. Often, however, the issue is often one of trade-offs, and how you lean depends on the purpose of your study. What do you really want or need to know? What amount of detail is necessary? For each item ask yourself:

1   *What information, exactly, am I going to get by designing it in this particular way?*
2   *Is that enough? Or do I want more detail—even perhaps something slightly different from what this item phrased in this way will get me?*

For example, note how each of these five questions asks for something slightly different:

How do *you feel* about our program?
What do *you like* about our program?
What do *you like best* about our program?
What is *most useful to you* about our program?
What do *you think* of our program?

Given the complexities of the human condition, social science measures never achieve 100 percent reliability and validity. It's simply too difficult to develop consensus on operational definitions across generations and cultures—and often, even, across individuals in the same profession. Without too much trouble we might develop a number of indicators that, when combined, provide a pretty reliable and valid overall measure of anger in children, for example. It's far more challenging to develop reliable and valid indicators for such concepts as *religiosity*, *bigotry*, *apathy*, *wellness*, and *illness* (and even for *mental illness* or *disorder*; note in particular the revisions in the 2013 *Diagnostic and Statistical Manual of Mental Disorders*, which will be superceded by a sixth version for this very reason). Even for such concepts in the social work profession as *practice*, *clinical*, *knowledge*, *evidence*, *therapy*, etc.—terms that are bandied about every day—were we to compare operational definitions, we would find enormous variation. The more you study concrete behavior, then, the easier it is to design highly reliable and valid instruments, although that stated, we do have an increasing number of sophisticated instruments to measure sophisticated concepts.

Still, remember that these are always subject to change/revision just as soon as the "next" theory comes about. Theories of human nature change. Just 20 years ago, we routinely asked people their race without qualm while today, we struggle to distinguish between race, ethnicity, and even culture. We also asked about sexual preference but today distinguish between sex and gender, identity and orientation, and self-concept and behavior. In short, what we think we know changes constantly. Is churchgoing a valid indicator of spirituality? It's certainly a reliable one; we'd all recognize churchgoing behavior if we saw it. But is it truly a sign of spirituality? That's not so clear. Perhaps it indicates sociability.

Working toward reliability: the rubber ruler pitfall

As noted briefly above, to work toward reliability is to work out the technical kinks in an instrument, which can be done in several ways (and to work out the kinks of the study process). You don't necessarily carry out all of them; the ones you choose to focus on make sense with respect to your study's purpose and design. Here are some ways to work toward a reliable measure (instrument):

1   Be very clear and specific in designing each item/question on the instrument and in the instructions.
2   Administer the same instrument twice to the same people and compare results (test/retest). The more similar they are, the more reliable the instrument.
3   Design two instruments (parallel forms) to measure one variable (e.g., bigotry). Give both to the same people, and compare results. If Mr. X reveals himself to be a bigot on both instruments, both tests are reliable.
4   If your instrument is large (e.g., 100 items) with duplicate items, split it into two equal halves, each containing items that go after the same data (split-half test). Carry out a parallel-forms test. The two halves can be assessed for equality through a coefficient alpha stat test.

5   Do everything possible to keep testing conditions equal for you and/or assistants (inter-rater/inter-observer reliability). Don't observe or interview some when you're alert and others when you're exhausted, for example.

6   Do everything possible to keep testing conditions as equal for participants (respondent reliability). Don't conduct some interviews in a private space and others in a public space or some when they have time and others when they're in a hurry, for example.

Working toward validity: getting to the heart of the matter

There are four types of validity to consider. However, you don't normally select one over the other. Again, the purpose of your study logically dictates which to consider most, although all instruments are expected to work toward construct validity (you'll see why later). So, review the purpose of your study, and read and reread your question or hypothesis. Then ask yourself:

1   *Am I interested in this instrument to predict the future of whoever responds to it?* If so, you're interested in *predictive validity*. Of course, instruments aren't always developed with this in mind, but such measures as GREs and SATs are.

    What do you do? You administer the instrument and wait to see what happens to the respondents in the future. If you get a positive correlation between their earlier scores on your instrument and future performance, the instrument can be said to have predictive validity. This kind of testing takes years.

2   *Am I interested in measuring differences among respondents now?* If so, you're interested in *concurrent validity*; you want to see how people vary in the present (as in knowledge, skill, attitude, etc.) What do you do? You use two different and feasible data collection methods to study the same thing (triangulation), such as observation and interviews.

    You want to study the way practitioners deal with conflict in client groups? Okay. In the interviews they describe their interventions. But how do you know they really do that? You don't. But if you then observe them in action, you can judge for yourself. If both the interview and observation indicate that they really do what they say, then both your interview guide and the checklist used for observation purposes have good concurrent validity. In other words, they each ask the right questions and get the real "scoop." If there are discrepancies, you need to rethink the instruments and data collection methods.

3   *Am I interested in using this instrument to measure (tap into/study) complex concepts?* If so, you're interested in *construct validity*. Social work is keenly interested in this type of validity; and most instruments intended to study complex phenomena are designed to work toward this type of validity.

As noted above, with a bit of work we could develop an observation checklist of indicators for apathy, for example, and then "go out and 'know' it when we 'see' it". To do so for its more complex social form, anomie, however, would be more difficult. Imagine the challenge of sending out ten assistants out into the world to not only seek out anomic social systems but then agreeing on anomie when they think they see it! Social science research is often interested in precisely these things, however.

So the dilemma is how to measure complex constructs when scientific standards require precise operational definitions (indicators). The answer is to anchor your indicators in a theoretical base (which you do by reviewing the literature). Anchoring your work in theory gives your study its greatest credibility and validity.

4 Finally, you ask yourself: *Can I even/at least achieve content validity?* Content validity refers to the logic of your instrument "on the face of it"—if, at the very least, it seems to measure what you want to measure. Often, exploratory studies go into such new territory that there is no real theoretical body of knowledge for anchoring questions and so construct validity is impossible to achieve. In that case, you locate as much expert feedback as possible about the nature and design of your questions or items, *on the face of it.*

In a nutshell, then, to work toward the reliability and validity of a research instrument means to work out both technical and conceptual kinks.

Major points to remember

- Measurement speaks to the reliability and validity of measures used to study something.
- Two rules of thumb: the clearer and more specific the questions and fewer the response categories, the higher the potential to achieve reliability; the subtler, the higher the potential to achieve validity.
- To work toward reliability is to work out technical kinks.
- To work toward validity is to work out conceptual kinks.
- It is difficult for social science measures to achieve 100 percent reliability and validity.

Exercise

Ask yourself

Write down some closed-ended questions/items that you'd want to include on an instrument to study your topic of interest, along with their response options (true/false, multiple choice, etc.). Now for each one ask yourself:

1   *Is it phrased as clearly as possible? Enough words? Too many words? The right words?* (Less is often more.)
2   *Is it really asking the question I want to ask?*
3   *Is the response option designed as clearly as possible?*

Then:

4   Show your questions to others for feedback.
5   Rework your questions/items.
6   Now for each one repeat Steps 2 through 5.

Yes, it's time consuming but well worth your effort!

Reference

American Psychiatric Association. (2013). *Diagnostic and Statistical Manual of Mental Disorders* (5th edn). Washington, DC: American Psychiatric Association.

18

SAMPLING

(Going to the source)

Key concepts

generalization
implications
nonrandom samples
populations
probability
randomization
random samples
sample frames

Introduction

Sample (v): (to sample …) to select elements (people, cases, objects) that conform to the criteria needed in order to participate in your study.

Sample (n): (a sample) the group of elements (people, cases, objects) that participates in your study.

A sample represents a portion of a population of interest to you (i.e., the total number of elements (people, cases, objects) that conform to some designated criteria). A population might be large or small and how that population is defined can vary from study to study. All MSW social workers in the United States might be a population of interest; all MSW social workers in New York State might be the population; all MSW social workers in New York City might be the population; all MSW social workers in the New York City Department of Child Welfare might be the population; or all MSW social workers in a private city organization who belong to the National Association of Social Workers (NASW) might be the population. You can imagine that the size of each of these populations varies tremendously in spite of their convergence on MSW social workers.

If every element (people, cases, objects) of a population was identical in every way, we wouldn't need to obtain samples; we'd simply study each one or the handiest, depending on size. That's rarely the case, however, except in certain program evaluation studies that may have access to all employees, for example, or all clients. In general, however, we use one of several possible sampling methods to develop a manageable group to study.

Going to the source

To go to the source is to go after the potential sources of information that will best give you the information you want, and the group composed of those sources is called your sample. Samples are said to be either probability or nonprobability samples.

Probability samples: forms and methods

Probability samples are so called because which elements from your population of interest end up in your sample is dictated by probability theory (aka chance). They're obtained through one of four possible random sampling methods. In research lingo random does not mean haphazard; it means that sample selection is dictated by laws of probability (theoretically, fair and unbiased), and not by you (generally unfair, even if subconsciously, and biased).

It's appropriate to use a probability sampling method when: (1) you can specify for each element its probability of being included in the sample; and (2) each element has an equal chance of being included in that sample. For example, every person in a population of 100 has an equal and known (1 percent) chance of being included in a final sample.

Probability samples are usually associated with descriptive, experimental, and correlational designs. The goal of working with a probability sample is to generalize your findings from it to its larger population. You simply obtained a small portion of a population to study because to study it in its entirety was unwieldy. You're still ultimately interested in knowing about the population as a whole, however. Thus, by keeping your fingers out of the process of who gets to participate and so reducing the potential for sample bias, probability samples permit generalization.

There are four types of probability samples: simple random, systematic random, stratified random, and cluster. The one you select depends on feasibility, the purpose of study, and how much control you're willing to let go of over who or what ends up in your sample. As you'll see, even within the "family" of probability methods, there are differences.

Simple random sample

This is the classic, most well-known type of sample and is the most reliable for making generalizations because who or what ends up in it is the most completely dictated by probability (i.e., the least interfered with by human hands) or, said conversely, least likely to be biased. It's often likened to picking numbers out of a hat.

Overview of method

1 Identify your population of interest (such as MSW social workers in New York City who are members of NASW).
2 Obtain a sampling frame, i.e., a roster of all the elements in that population (such as a current roster of NYC NASW members).
3 Assign each element a number beginning with 1. (Thus, the first name becomes 1, the second 2, the third 3, etc.).
4 Decide on sample size (e.g., out of a sampling frame of 1,000 a final sample of 100). There are no hard and fast rules around size, but 30 elements is the very minimum for statistical analysis. The bigger the better, as long as it doesn't become unwieldy.
5 Use a table of random numbers (in every research or stats book or many computer statistical programs) to select the 100 elements for your final sample. How? Easy. The first 100 four-digit numbers (in order to give no. 1,000 a chance too) you come to in a table of random numbers that match the numbers of your elements or identified by the computer program become your sample.

Strengths and weaknesses

This sample type offers the greatest potential for generalization because of all the methods, sample membership is most dictated by probability theory and thus least potentially biased. However, it can be unwieldy to use with huge numbers. Even with a computer program to identify random numbers, you may have to assign the initial number to every element in the sampling frame by hand. The next method is often used as a good alternative.

Systematic random sample

This method is less complicated, because you don't have to assign a number to each element or use a table of random numbers.

Overview of method

1 Identify your population of interest (such as MSW social workers in New York City who are members of NASW).

2 Obtain a sampling frame, i.e., a roster of all the elements in that population (such as a current roster of NYC NASW members).

3 Decide on sample size (e.g., out of a sampling frame of 1,000 a final sample of 100). There are no hard and fast rules around size, but 30 elements is the very minimum for statistical analysis. The bigger the better, as long as it doesn't become unwieldy.

4 Develop your sample by selecting every nth element on the sampling frame until you have enough (100). To know what "every nth element" is you divide the sampling frame total (1,000) by your final sample (100). Here, then, the "nth" interval is ten; so you'd select every tenth element to end up with 100.

5 How to pick the first? Anywhere before your first "nth" (here, ten). Use a table of random numbers (or throw dice or pick a number from one to n out of a hat, etc.); the number you get is your first sample member; the others are at every nth interval thereafter.

Strengths and weaknesses

This method is easier to use than simple random. Its major disadvantage is the possibility that some unknown order is operating on your sampling frame and introducing a bias. Say the sampling frame is cyclical in a way that coincides with your nth interval (e.g., it has a five-element cycle but you don't know it, and you're choosing every fifth element); it's possible that you'll draw a grossly biased sample.

Stratified random sample

This sample is developed to make sure desired categories of elements are represented. This method, then, combines some reliance on probability theory with some control by you, because you don't completely trust chance to give you good representation through either simple or systematic methods.

Overview of method

1 Identify your population of interest (such as MSW social workers in New York City who are members of NASW).

2 Obtain a sampling frame, i.e., a roster of all the elements in that population (such as a current roster of NYC NASW members).

3 Decide on sample size (e.g., out of a sampling frame of 1,000 a final sample of 100). There are no hard and fast rules around size, but 30 elements is the very minimum for statistical analysis. The bigger the better, as long as it doesn't become unwieldy.

4 Divide sampling frame into strata that are mutually exclusive on a variable that you want particularly represented. Let's say it is age group for your study. You

then develop stratum one for persons under 40; stratum two for persons from 41 to 60; and stratum three for persons 61 and older.

5   Simple or systematic sample each stratum—for example, 33 from one, 33 from two, 34 from three. If one stratum is much larger than the other/s, you can pick proportionately to have more of one and less of another. Often, for example, strata of females are larger than those of males. Thus, you might decide to get 65 subjects from a female stratum and 35 from a male stratum. This is called weighting.

6   Combine the elements from each stratum into a final sample.

Strengths and weaknesses

This method ensures representation along certain variables, particularly when the sampling frame may include gross differences—often the case for race, gender, or age group, for example. By increasing your control, however (by not letting probability theory completely dictate the sample), you also increase the potential for bias.

Cluster sample

Much social science research involves the study of mega populations for which it's difficult to obtain sampling frames, such as the residents of a very large city or for large categories, such as all college students in the United States or all Florida churchgoers. In these cases, cluster sampling is an option. Cluster sampling typically involves two sampling levels: an initial sampling of groups or "clusters" followed by a secondary sampling of individual elements (e.g., persons). It can, of course, involve more than two clusters, particularly with enormous populations.

Overview of method

1   Identify your population of interest (e.g., all churchgoers in Florida).

2   Obtain an initial sampling frame of groups or "clusters," in this case a list of discrete churches in that state.

3   Decide on an initial sample size. Let's say there are 5,000 discrete churches in Florida. They're your initial sampling frame. And let's say you decide on 500 churches.

4   From the list of 5,000 churches you use simple, systematic, or stratified random sampling to select the initial sample (500 churches).

5   You then obtain a secondary sampling frame, in this case lists from the 500 churches of their individual members. These lists of individual members are your secondary sampling frame (let's say the 500 lists contain 20,000 names).

6   You then use simple, systematic, or stratified random sampling to select the final sample (say 2,000 individuals).

7   You can add more levels (such as sampling a city for zoning areas, sampling zoning areas for blocks, and sampling the blocks for households, etc.) until you pare down to the actual unit you want to study.

Strengths and weaknesses

Cluster sampling makes it possible to study large and unruly things by breaking them down into something more manageable. While it's very efficient because it moves you from the cosmic to the workable, however, you do increase the potential for sample bias. Every time you carry out a probability-sampling process, it is said to be subject to one sample error (a way of acknowledging the inevitable humanity factor in all we do). Thus, with one level of sampling you're already subject to one sampling error; with cluster sampling, of course, you're subject to at least two sampling errors and possibly more if you add more levels.

Recap of basic advantages of probability samples

In sum, the basic advantages to probability sampling are as follows:

1   Probability sampling helps to rule out human biases that might be involved in more casual selection.
2   Probability sampling enhances the likelihood of accurate representation by letting probability (aka chance) determine your sample.
3   The reliance of probability sampling on probability theory lets you estimate the degree of error you can expect with your sample. The smaller the error the better.

A note of caution: if you end up with a sample quite different from your original one (because, for example, some people never returned your questionnaire or dropped out of a program you're testing or who you've been observing become unavailable for further observation), your ability to generalize diminishes.

Nonprobability samples: forms and methods

Nonprobability samples are obtained through one of three possible nonrandom sampling methods. It's appropriate to use nonrandom methods when: (1) there's no way to estimate the probability of inclusion for any one element; or (2) you can't make sure they all have an equal chance of being included in the first place.

Nonrandom sampling is usually associated with exploratory design. Why? Because when there's little known about a subject, you aren't picky about how you get the information, and your methodological priority becomes getting at that information. The ultimate goal of working with a nonprobability sample is to develop implications for action or further thought and study, although each of the three methods takes a slightly different approach to exploration.

Size of sample is less of an issue in nonprobability forms than for probability forms, which are intended to permit generalization. While the rule of thumb for probability samples is a very minimum of 30 cases, then (although that's not always possible in some experimental designs, for example), the rule of thumb for nonprobability samples is that there must be some logic between the research question and consideration of sample size and that data yield must be rich in quality. Some studies explore single cases, while studies that seek variety in perspective (as in the viewpoints of upper and middle management, line workers, and support staff) need larger numbers.

Accidental (aka convenience) sample

This type of sample is composed simply of the elements (cases, people, etc.) at hand, whoever or whatever is easily available, such as the first ten people to walk in the room or to pass through the train station or to be willing to answer you (e.g., a "man on the street" approach).

Overview of method

1   Identify the best (i.e., most efficient, most effective) context for having the right cases at hand to answer your research question.
2   Decide on sample size.
3   Develop a data collection plan (i.e., how and when to go to the site and how to get the information you need—see Chapter 19).
4   Carry out a pilot test (i.e., enter the context to assess the likelihood of its yielding both the quality and quantity of data you seek).
5   Implement the study.

Strengths and weaknesses

This method allows us to study groups and phenomena that might not otherwise be available or accessible. Its primary weakness is its potential for sample bias, although that is to some extent a moot issue because generalization is not a priority.

Quota sample

Like stratified random sampling, quota sampling identifies desired characteristics and then ensures that cases with those characteristics are included in the sample. In contrast, however, elements are selected purposely. That is, you don't use any random sampling but just go after cases with that characteristic until it's "well enough" represented. Are you concerned that males be represented in your sample? Then make sure you go after what you consider to be "enough" male participants.

Overview of method

1   Identify which participant/case characteristics are crucial to your sample.
2   Decide on sample size.
3   Develop a data collection plan (i.e., how you're going to get the information you need—see Chapter 19).
4   Identify and get the information desired from cases that will yield good representation around the characteristics identified.

Strengths and weaknesses

This method ensures representation along certain variables of importance. It's not fruitful to recruit very small samples this way, however, because the smaller it is the less heterogeneity has real meaning. For example, it's less reasonable to draw inferences about gender in a sample of ten with five men and five women than in one of 30 with 15 men and 15 women. (Thus, it would be also unreasonable to draw inferences about gender if the final sample consisted of 25 women and five men because of the low degree of male representation.) This method also has the potential to be grossly biased, making it important to consider and report all aspects of context, such as geographic location, age range, or perhaps racial or religious or cultural composition of the sample, etc. Like all nonprobability methods, however, it can identify variables, create implications, and provide valuable food for further thought and study.

Purposive (aka judgmental) sample

This sample consists of purposely selected elements (cases, persons, objects) because of their particular characteristics, either (1) extreme, such as known experts or pioneers in a field, or (2) typical, such as people with a certain illness or social situation of interest. Quota samples are also purposive to the extent that you select "enough" cases with certain characteristics; but purposive samples are drawn from an available population without stratifying first.

For example, you might seek out expert researchers to help you formulate your research problem, gain theoretical insights, or identify potentially important concepts. In these cases you would purposely seek them out for their ability to help you rather than because of their gender or age range, etc. You might also seek out practitioners who are expert at working with certain groups or problems. And in some cases, those experts also may be "typical." Practitioners are experts about their approach to practice, but they also reflect typical cases of persons whose behavior you want to study.

Overview of method

1   Identify the best sources for obtaining the information needed to answer your research question (either experts or typical cases).
2   Decide on sample size.
3   Develop a data collection plan (i.e., how you're going to get the information you need—see Chapter 19).

Strengths and weaknesses

This method ensures representation either in expertise or object, increasing your ability to get your questions answered. And here, bias is a good thing. Why? Because you want sample members to be extreme (expert), or you want them to be typical objects of interest. In other words, you want your sample to be biased in a certain direction—to have an expertise or reputable "judgment" about your area of interest. Once again, its weakness is that, like other nonprobability methods, it doesn't permit generalization. Your findings must remain contextual, i.e., about the sample itself. Once again, however, generalization is not its ultimate goal.

Recap of basic advantages of nonprobability samples

In sum, the major reasons for using nonprobability sampling methods are that:

1   Nonprobability sampling is convenient.
2   You can make choices of inclusion/exclusion with nonprobability sampling in a way that advances the feasibility of your study.
3   You don't have to go through a complex randomization or computerization process with nonprobability sampling.
4   Nonprobability sampling is efficient, generally needing less time and money than a random selection process.
5   Nonprobability sampling makes it possible to access populations that would be otherwise impossible to reach and for which it would be even more impossible to develop a sampling frame, such as homeless persons in a large city or underground cultures.

Major points to remember

- To sample is to select elements (people, cases, objects) to participate in your study.
- A sample is that group of elements that participates in your study.
- A sample is a piece of a population of interest (total number of elements) that conform to some criteria, such as age range, gender, geographic location, professional degree, etc.
- Probability theory dictates membership in probability samples. You dictate membership in nonprobability samples.

- A probability sample, obtained through one of four possible random sampling methods, is appropriate when you can specify for each element its probability of being included and when each element has an equal chance of being included.
- A nonprobability sample, obtained through one of three possible nonrandom sampling methods, is appropriate when you have no way of estimating the probability of inclusion for any element or can't make sure they all have an equal chance of inclusion.
- Generally speaking, the ultimate goal of using a probability sample is generalization, while the ultimate goal of using a nonprobability sample is to have access to information in the first place.
- Probability samples are generally associated with descriptive, experimental, and correlational studies. Nonprobability samples are generally associated with exploratory studies.
- The purpose of your study generally suggests a sampling method, although real-world factors, such as cost, inability to get a sampling frame, etc., can require redirection.

Exercise

Sample a sample

So, you have a research problem? It's stated in a sentence form that's clear enough to repeat nonchalantly when people ask about it? And you've also got the design down pat (sort of)? But now you need a source of information? Okay, ask yourself:

1 *Does a probability sample make sense for the study I have in mind? Why/Why not?*
2 *Does a nonprobability sample make sense for the study I have in mind? Why/Why not?*
3 *If a probability sample, which of the following four makes most sense and why?*
   - *Simple random*
   - *Systematic random*
   - *Stratified random*
   - *Cluster*
4 *Would my choice be feasible? If so, how would a selection process actually look? If not, then what?*
5 *If a nonprobability sample, which of the following three makes most sense and why?*
   - *Accidental*
   - *Quota*
   - *Purposive*
6 *Would my choice be feasible? If so, how would a selection process actually look? If not, then what?*

19

DATA COLLECTION

(Getting to the answers)

Key concepts

interview
objectivity
observation
person-in-situation
questionnaire
reliability
self-report
specificity
structure
subjectivity
survey
validity

Introduction

There are three major data collection methods: observation, interviews, and questionnaires. Each one has several possible variations, and studies often combine methods. The methods are presented here in terms of advantages and disadvantages; which to select depends theoretically on the purpose of your study and in real-world terms on such factors as access, expense, etc. The method most commonly associated with questionnaires is the *survey*, an instrument usually composed of primarily closed-ended questions and designed to reach a large number of respondents.

In each case it's important to consider the vulnerability of the population you're studying (also see Chapter 2 on ethics). The more vulnerable it is the less you should assume that a signed *Informed Consent* form truly reflects consent. Many things may compel people to accommodate your request, including a sense of power differential and a desire to avoid negative repercussions that may accompany a refusal. Thus, interviewing colleagues, for example, is one thing; interviewing people we call clients is another altogether.

Observation

Advantages

- You can "see" (notice, observe) things for yourself.
- You can see behaviors in their natural settings.
- You don't have to rely on self-reporting.
- You don't usually have to prepare lots of materials.
- You can use this method with all populations regardless of their literary or verbal skills.
- You don't have to rely on willingness to participate.

Disadvantages

- There is high potential for subjective interpretation on the part of the observer/s.
- There is high potential for rater/inter-rater bias.
- Your presence may contaminate the setting or situation and result in questionable validity of whatever is being observed.
- You can only observe the "here and now" and only draw inferences about the past or future.
- Observation can be time consuming and expensive.

Issues to consider

1   Because there's a high potential for subjective interpretation, observers must be well trained to keep that kind of bias to a minimum. Also, the high potential for rater and inter-rater bias may make it difficult to evaluate and/or code the results.
2   There are some ways to control a bit for the potential that your presence contaminates the setting and thus to increase the validity of what's being observed. For example, you might spend time in the observation context to get people used to seeing you in the hope that whatever behavioral changes might still occur because of your initial presence eventually diminish.
3   Sometimes it seems as if informed consent for observation will interfere with the purpose of the study (that there's a need to see behavior in authentic vivo, for example, or that high-status or powerful people may not want to be observed), causing a real tension between the ethics of informed consent and

need for information. Even if other fields argue in favor of "need to know," however, professional values of individual autonomy and self-determination take some precedence in social work research. See the NASW *Code of Ethics* as a guide.

Interviews

Advantages

- You control the process to get exactly the information you want.
- You can get to complex issues.
- You can clarify questions and responses.
- You can make both the format (how you do what you do) and process (what you do) as rigid or flexible as you wish.
- You can observe the "person (or process, dynamic, etc.) in situation."
- You can use interviews with illiterate persons.
- You have access to nonverbal cues.
- It is easier to get people's cooperation for interviews than for written narratives outside your presence.
- You have a high response rate because you control the process.

Disadvantages

- Your presence may affect (i.e., bias) the situation or the setting (such as eliciting socially desirable responses).
- Your personality may affect (i.e., bias) the situation.
- The quality of your interaction may have unwanted effects on responses.
- Conducting interviews can be expensive and time consuming.

Issues to consider

1 How to know when the interview is over, other than the fact that the time is running out? Here's a rule of thumb: when you think the person has "said it all," ask for a bit more. When he or she starts repeating him or herself, you're probably done.

2 Your personality, the quality of your interaction, and even your mere presence may bias the process, so maintain as neutral a presence as possible. This doesn't mean aloof; it means cordial, even friendly, but without judgment as you ask questions and hear answers. The only facial expression you should don is one that shows interest and attention. Use your practice skills.

3 Don't hit and run! Give people a chance to brief and to debrief. A few moments to make sure the person is prepared for the interview and a few moments to talk freely afterward will benefit both of you. You can also use

debriefing time to ask about the possibility of a feedback session, when you can take your analysis and interpretations back for confirmation.

4   Be polite! The respondent is helping you, regardless of your subject. Don't take an aggressive mindset, even if you're asking about issues on which your opinions, attitudes, or feelings are different from those of the interviewee. It's only because he or she is willing to talk with you that you've got a study going, no matter what you think of the responses! If you do feel aggressive, let someone else do the interview, or choose another method!

5   Finally, if you're asking people to talk about things that require a lot of thought, consider sending them a copy of your interview guide ahead of time. Remember, your purpose isn't to meet with them and "trick" them into a quick, off-the-cuff response. It's to acquire thoughtful and deliberately considered narrative material in response to your questions.

Questionnaires (surveys)

Advantages

*   Questionnaires can be highly reliable.
*   Questionnaires have the potential for a high degree of validity if they allow respondents time and privacy to think through their responses.
*   Because they are standardized, questionnaires are usually easy to analyze.
*   Questionnaires allow study of the past and future as well as the "here and now."
*   Questionnaires are relatively inexpensive and easy to administer to large numbers or to survey a wide geographic area.

Disadvantages

*   Highly structured questionnaires may force people into categories that do not accurately reflect them.
*   Questionnaires do not allow clarification, expansion, or explanation by either researcher or respondent (unless administered in person, in which case other issues may impinge on the nature and/or yield of information).
*   Questionnaires require some degree of literacy.
*   People must be able to express themselves in writing.
*   There's no opportunity to observe nonverbal communication (unless administered in person, in which case other issues may impinge on the nature and/or yield of information).

Issues to consider

1   Designing a questionnaire that's both highly reliable and captures the full flavor of respondents' positions (valid) isn't an easy task, so if you're not using

one already available, consider the time it will take to design it, field test (pilot test) it, and rework it until it's both reliable and valid. Don't do this alone. Get feedback on the design and testing process from others in the know.

2   Remember that highly structured questionnaires don't allow either you or the respondent any opportunity to clarify or expand on questions or answers (either in writing, verbally, or nonverbally); so design your items with that in mind.

3   Because questionnaires have such a low return rate, be sure to distribute many more than you need as a final sample.

Express your gratitude!

Regardless of method, find a way to offer a heartfelt thank you to participants! This may have to be "up front" with surveys/questionnaires (either in the introductory narrative or at the very end of the survey), but however it works best for your study, don't forget to do it. After all, your respondents will have given you their valuable time just to help you out! Yes, of course, they may benefit from knowing that they are contributing to an increase of knowledge on a particular topic, but still … it's so much easier to just throw a questionnaire in the wastebasket! So don't forget about this.

Major points to remember

- The three major data collection methods are observation, interviews, and questionnaires.
- Each method has possible variations, and studies often combine them.
- Which method to select depends in theory on the purpose of your study and in real-world terms on feasibility.

Exercise

From theory to the real world

So data collection is where theory meets the real world—where you determine exactly how you're going to do what you need to do to get your answers. As you begin this process, ask yourself:

1   *As exactly as possible, what information do I need to best answer my research question as it's formulated?*

2   *What setting/situation/context is going to be most conducive to my getting the information I'm after? Do I need to observe behavior? Am I looking for a fringe or invisible or underground population? Do I want people to sit and talk with me? Am I more likely to get the information I need through anonymity? Where and how might I find the sample I'm interested in to get the information I need?*

Whichever the case, even if it is tentative, think about the purpose of your study and ask yourself:

- *Does this method make the most sense? Why or why not? Consider political and strategic issues, costs, access, privacy factors, ethics, etc.*
- *To what extent will this method influence the findings I get? Will they be so idiosyncratic that they won't present much food for thought for other contexts? And if so, will that be okay? Why or why not? If not, then what?*
- *Should I get the information I need from people who are the objects of my study or from others? In either case, why or why not?*

3   *Should I be the (only) one to collect data? Why or why not? What impact will I (or assistant researchers) have on the method I have in mind?* (This might range from very low [as in, *Well, you could say that my world view or general perspective is what made me choose this subject*] to very high [as in, *Well, I think my presence would have a great impact because I'll be very visible as an observer …*]).

4   *If my presence (or that of assistants) is likely to have an impact, would that be acceptable to me given the purpose of my study? Why or why not? If not, then what?*

20

DATA ANALYSIS: AN OVERVIEW

(Okay, you've got the answers ... now what?)

Key concepts

constructivism
content analysis
logical positivism
meaning
mixed methods
qualitative
quantitative
significance

Introduction

To analyze data is to make meaning of your results, both descriptively (what they are) and interpretively (what they indicate, suggest, imply, etc.). It is, in short, to complete a kind of puzzle that, when finished, tells a story about your sample and, depending on the type of your design, proposes a story for the population from which you drew that sample.

Qualitative data analysis

Qualitative data refers to material collected in the form of written words (and, with technology, the spoken word as well); and qualitative data analysis, usually associated with exploratory studies, consists of content analysis, i.e., analyzing the written word, sometimes called narratives or stories. Qualitative data is at the heart of exploratory studies, but it is also often included in one way or other in all types of studies. For example, even a large-scale survey now and then will have an essay box at the end for other comments—comments that the respondent may wish to make either about the survey itself or about some aspect of the question it seeks to answer. When both quantitative and qualitative data are sought on a relatively equal footing (that is, one type of data is not subservient to the other), such a study is often referred to as *mixed methods*.

To carry out qualitative analysis is to do a lot of work both during and after implementation in the form of content analysis as each narrative is transcribed and analyzed. This kind of analysis takes place as the data collection occurs, not afterward, so that, for example, each interview is analyzed on its own before being compared to and contrasted with others, helping the researcher gain insights with each one that may cause a slight variation in the next (such as a new seemingly important question).

For interviews, a common form of qualitative data collection, two primary sources for organizing qualitative data are: (1) the questions on the interview guide; and (2) the insights that emerge as you collect and/or analyze the data (this is the part where you reflect on each interview [or piece of literature, for example] before reviewing and reflecting on the next). It's acceptable to begin with either, and it's fine to change your mind along the way; in fact, it would be crazy not to change your organizing framework if the one you're using begins to make less sense while another one takes shape! Those new to research often organize their findings in a linear fashion according to questions that were asked, but it is more often the case than not that larger themes emerge as one reflects on those findings, suggesting a different way to organize the final report. *Ethnography*, *ethnomethodology*, *content analysis*, *narrative analysis*, *conversation analysis*, *grounded theory analysis*, *case-oriented analysis* ... you will find these and more such references to approaches to analysis that seek out and seek to understand text or language. The most generic reference to these types of analysis is *content analysis*. Read more about qualitative data analysis in Chapter 21.

Quantitative data analysis

The term *quantitative data* (data is plural, by the way) refers to material collected in actual numerical form (as in number of years) or to which we've assigned numerical codes (as in multiple-choice codes, e.g., A __ yes, B __ no, and C __ maybe).

Quantitative data analysis, usually associated with large-scale descriptive studies, experiments, and correlational studies, consists of understanding numbers (statistics) in two ways: (1) as they describe your findings (how people responded) and, thus, the salient characteristics of your sample; and (2) as they help you to infer the significance (degree of reality/truth/accuracy) of your findings for the sample itself (its story) and the extent to which you can confidently generalize those findings to the population from which you drew your sample (the question being, *Is that same story likely to apply to the population?*).

Statistics

Statistics? They're simply numbers that help us make meaning of quantitative data. Descriptive statistics ("stats") give a summary look at sample characteristics and responses. Inferential stats, which are based on descriptive stats, help us to determine the significance of our quantitative findings.

To carry out quantitative analysis is to spend a lot of time designing or choosing an appropriate standardized instrument (so, front-heavy labor), with a fairly easy go of it later on, when analysis consists of examining and interpreting numbers (the actual statistical analysis being often assigned to a statistician and returned for interpretation). To make meaning of quantitative data, therefore, is to use statistics to summarize, organize, describe, and interpret your findings.

Using descriptive statistics

Descriptive stats summarize your data in visual nutshells through tables, charts, and graphs. Some visuals offer a blow-by-blow description of each item/question (variable), called univariate analysis (as in gender, age, religious affiliation, number of siblings, years in practice). Some describe how (if) two items/questions (variables) relate to each other in your sample, called bivariate analysis (as in how each gender as a group responded to the question on religious affiliation, etc.). And some describe how (if) three or more items/questions (variables) relate to one another, called multivariate analysis (as in gender by age range by religious affiliation).

Read more about descriptive stats in Chapter 22.

Using inferential statistics

Based on various laws of probability, inferential stats tell you how confidently you can infer that your quantitative findings are probably a real/true/accurate reflection of your sample (not a chance thing or due to sampling error), and how confidently you can infer a resemblance between your sample and the population from which you drew it. Why all this need for inference? Because after data collection you only have numbers (stats) for your sample, not for everyone the sample is supposed to represent, remember?

So what? So now you need to use what you know about the smaller group (sample) to learn about the larger group (population), because that was your goal in the first place. You decided to learn about a large group by studying a small piece of it. So now you must back your way into knowing that larger group, so to speak, through inference. And that's what inferential stats do; based on your sample's descriptive stats, they help you determine if your sample findings "hold water" for the larger group as well.

Inferential stats come from various mathematical formulas called tests of statistical significance, which are based on your descriptive stats. They're selected according to the level of measure (LOM) of the variable/s in question and whether you're looking at difference or association; and they result in certain numbers (stats), each of which tells you something about your potential for inference.

Read more about inferential stats in Chapter 23 and significance testing in Chapter 24.

The great debate: qualitative versus quantitative

For years on end, arguments have taken place over the scientific legitimacy of qualitative data on one hand and the practical utility or even validity of quantitative data on the other.

The heart of the argument for quantitative data is that nothing short of replicating so-called hard-science principles (rationality, objectivity, etc.) and methods (including quantification of all variables, often referred to as "hard" data) is acceptable. The proponents of this approach are referred to as logical positivists (or, as identified by some, contemporary positivists); their tickets to knowledge are objectivity and quantification.

The opposing "camp" has argued that the fluidity of human nature makes it impossible to study it through only quantitative means and that, even further, in attempting to understand the human condition, subjectivity plays just as important a role in the world (perhaps even a greater one) as so-called objectivity. The proponents of this approach are referred to as constructivists (also called interpretivists by some); their ticket to knowledge is understanding the meanings that people attach to their world.

There are also numerous labels to describe positions on the spectrum that fall in between these two extremes (where most reasonable minds meet), including that group of inquirers whose approach to science is specific to goals of empowerment and/or social action.

What a waste of breath to argue who or which is more valuable! Clearly, there's need and room for many approaches depending on nature of inquiry, context, purpose, etc. To debate what is "real" science is to misdirect attention to status instead of substance. Good quantitative studies offer what qualitative data cannot, and vice versa. Well-rounded pictures of anything always include many aspects or angles. Census reports offer interesting numbers about who's doing what where, and stories of tradition and culture, for example, offer interesting food for thought about who's doing what to whom, where, and why. And as social workers, if we are particularly interested in scientific inquiry toward social justice, then let's go ahead!

In a nutshell, don't waste your energy on this kind of debate. If the purpose of your study (or what you are seeking) suggests that it makes sense to go after quantitative data, do it. If the purpose of your study (or what you are seeking) suggests that it makes sense to go after qualitative data, do it. In truth, most studies mix their methods, seeking both quantitative data (e.g., demographics and other characteristics of a sample for a so-called qualitative study) and qualitative data (e.g., spaces for open-ended short-answer or essay-type responses on so-called quantitative measures).

Major points to remember

- To analyze data is to make meaning of results, both descriptively and interpretively.
- Qualitative data analysis is usually associated with exploratory studies and consists of analyzing the written (or spoken) word. *Ethnography, ethnomethodology, content analysis, narrative analysis, conversation analysis, grounded theory analysis, case-oriented analysis* … you will find these and more such references to approaches to analysis that seek out and seek to understand text or language. The most generic reference to these types of analysis is *content analysis*.
- Quantitative data analysis is usually associated with large-scale descriptive, experimental, or correlational studies and consists of understanding numbers that describe your findings or those that tell you about the capacity to generalize.
- To carry out qualitative analysis is to expect a lot of work during and after implementation.
- To carry out quantitative analysis is to spend a lot of time in designing or choosing an appropriate standardized instrument, which means front-heavy labor.
- Analysis, description, and interpretation of qualitative data all revolve around the purpose of a study, which provides the context for making meaning, usually to the end of theory building.
- To make meaning of quantitative data is to use numbers to summarize, organize, describe, and interpret your findings.
- Both qualitative and quantitative data have value in social work research, and, more often than not, studies seek both types of data in order to capture as full a "picture" of and tell as comprehensive a "story" as possible for the study sample and, in some cases, for the population from which it was drawn.

Exercise

Get directions

So by now your study should be taking shape. What direction seems to make sense to you?

1   Does it look like you are moving toward an exploratory study? If so, then you're probably most interested in (*random/nonrandom*) sampling, right? And in collecting primarily (*qualitative/quantitative*) data, right? And in carrying out (*content/statistical*) analysis, right?

2   Or does it look you are headed toward a descriptive study? If so, then you're probably most interested in (*random/nonrandom*) sampling, right? And in collecting primarily (*qualitative/quantitative*) data, right? And in carrying out (*content/statistical*) analysis, right?

3   Or does it look like you might actually conduct an experiment? If so, then you're probably most interested in (*random/nonrandom*) sampling, right? And in collecting primarily (*qualitative/quantitative*) data, right? And in carrying out (*content/statistical*) analysis, right?

4   Or does it look like a correlation design of some type may have to suffice? If so, then you're probably most interested in (*random/nonrandom*) sampling, right? And in collecting primarily (*quantitative/qualitative*) data, right? And in carrying out (*content/statistical*) analysis, right?

5   Or perhaps you're thinking about evaluating your practice? If so, kudos to you! How might you get your sample (N = 1)? What kind of (*quantitative/qualitative*) data will you primarily collect and why? And then you'll carry out (*content/statistical*) data analysis, right?

6   Or finally, perhaps you are brave enough to conduct a piece of program evaluation. In that case, you'll probably go for a (*random/nonrandom*) sample, right? And then you'll collect primarily (*quantitative/qualitative*) data, right? Why so? And finally you'll carry out (*content/statistical*) data analysis, right?

21

QUALITATIVE DATA ANALYSIS: MAKING SENSE OF WORDS

(How many pages to look at?)

Key concepts

audience
bias
coding
completeness
confirmability
content analysis
context
evidence
grounded theory
qualitative data
saturation
self–reflection
thick description
transferability
truth
utility

Introduction

Qualitative analysis, or analysis of words, written or spoken, is referred to in its most basic form as *content analysis*; and its central task is to understand, interpret, and represent the meaning of what has been said. There are several types of analysis; content analysis is the basic/generic reference, because you are analyzing the content (both explicit and implicit) of text or perhaps the spoken word, especially as technology makes it possible to audio record the transmission of information.

Depending on your perspective, you might even include nonverbal communication (approaching it, for example, as a form of narrative rather than behavior, as it is traditionally conceptualized). Furthermore, the range of material to be analyzed is almost endless, including anything that contains language. You might be interested in historical materials or archival documents, agency policies, written or audio recordings of speeches, case records, and on and on—including the professional literature that is sometimes reviewed not only as a step in formulating a problem but also as an end, in and of itself.

So if you're interested in the kind of study that calls for this kind of analysis, expect to spend a great deal of time on analysis! Finally, remember that analysis, description, and interpretation of qualitative data all revolve around the purpose of your study. Why you want to know what you want to know provides the context for making meaning of the data and usually does so to the end of theory building— some overall story about your sample (of persons, cases, objects, articles, etc.).

Perhaps most crucial to this process is the researcher's awareness of personal biases, ranging from those that direct him or her toward a certain topic in the first place to those that tend to hide out in the back of his or her mind as analysis takes place.

Analysis begins by developing clarity about the narrative itself—by understanding the words as set forth. (Actually, it begins with a feeling for the flavor of their context as the environment and nonverbal cues are assessed if they result from interviews, and as field notes or memos written afterward as records of that assessment are also analyzed). It continues with some assessment of their greater meaning—the larger stories they tell.

Developing those stories is the interpretive piece of content analysis. Some stories are rather straightforward, but often they're obscure and require some artistic "reading between the lines" or extrapolation, which is why the concept of evidence, which refers to the narrator's own words, is so central to content analysis.

Here's an important rule of thumb as you begin analysis, then: each and every time you move from description of what has been said to interpretation, you provide solid evidence (direct quotes) to back it up.

Mindset: the truth about truth

People new to qualitative analysis often worry that respondents may not tell the "truth." Well, what constitutes "truth" is a long and honorable question; and when you go after people's stories, you do, in fact, get their perspectives of what constitutes the "truth" (their truth, as they see it, which is what you are after, yes?). Reaching for truth in a common-sense way in analysis is important, of course, but truth is always in the eyes of the storyteller when you're reaching for narrative material. And that's not a bad thing. In fact, that's what you're after. You're after people's stories—how they see or saw things; and they are the rightful authors of those stories. So better to focus your energy on your ability to interpret and represent those stories accurately. In fact, your ability to be a "truthful" (i.e., reliable) reporter is probably in greater question than that of your participants. Think for a moment. Researchers (funded in one way or another) probably have more reasons than anyone else to slant their findings, no?

Since truth and perspective are often matters of degree, then, focus on your own ability for truth; be prepared to provide in writing what's often called a "thick description" of everything you did, who you did it to, and why you did it that way; and then let others judge the credibility (truth) of your interpretations and applicability of your findings. This means you describe your methods (including all process details and obstacles); the nature and characteristics of your sample (including how and why you selected it and why it is the size it is); and how you analyzed your data and why you did it that way. (Anticipate lots of page space!) In fact, assume that your notes will be seen by others (someone who wishes to analyze your methods, for example). And think utility. Work hard to make your findings apply to the real world—in real situations to real people with real problems.

Whoa! You have to tell all? Bare all? Leave yourself open to criticism? Yes. Right. Secrecy has no place in research. And since you have such power over shaping the story that comes from qualitative material (in contrast to numbers, which more easily speak for themselves), you have the most potential for being "untruthful"—that is, for letting your biases get in the way of accuracy, even if inadvertently.

Issues to consider

1   As you begin, remember your intended audience, and develop implications for that audience. If there are more than one, speak clearly to each one.

2   Consider transferability. That is, be clear about where and when your findings do and might apply. Use examples to distinguish between the two; don't leave consumers to figure it out alone. The history of research is too replete with misinterpretation!

3   Complement but don't reshape findings by interpretation, using lots of evidence to back it up. Provide meaning in context, conveying the gestalt of your data; in fact, acknowledging context is a strength of qualitative studies. Keep interpretations contextual (to your sample only). That is, think confirmability. Offer many examples, get reports from primary sources, get feedback sessions if possible, and leave an explicit audit trail in writing for others to follow your process in their minds' eye.

4   Present findings as exhaustively as possible. How to know? When your coding scheme seems to have captured all aspects of each major issue, it's saturated. And when your analysis reflects not only major themes as you see them but variations and contradictions, the picture is complete.

5   Work hard to limit your biases through active self-reflection. Consciously think about them; make them explicit; get feedback on interpretations from others. Don't get attached to a certain way of coding or early interpretation;

stay open to change as analysis progresses. Keep other biases in mind too, such as those of funding sources, and be sure to identify them in your report.

Carrying out the analysis

There are different models of qualitative data analysis, and a few moments in the library or bookstore or surfing the internet will identify a number of possible sources to learn more about them in general or any one in particular. Here are the basic steps of the grounded theory method of analysis, a commonly used model (Glaser and Strauss 1967).

In essence, qualitative data analysis consists of:

1   *Intra-transcript analysis*: try to make meaning of each transcript (transcript referring, for example, to the verbatim notes taken during an interview, audio or video recorded and typed up afterward, or the place on a questionnaire that was left for respondents to offer written comments). What is the respondent saying or trying to say, do you think? Note each thing (theme, subject, issue, reference) of apparent importance whenever it comes up again in the transcript (like circling a phrase or paragraph), and use a label or code to note it in the margin. Look for quotes that provide direct evidence of what you think you're hearing, and seek both positive and negative examples, e.g.:

> *Mrs. Jones often talked about the quality of her early education in public school.*

The fact that a reference to something is brought up only once does not mean that it isn't important. One respondent might raise an issue that strikes you as extremely important (relevant, etc.)—something about which you had never thought in this context but because of your professional knowledge now seems obvious or very salient to practice. So think about the quality of what you're reading, not necessarily about only quantity (how often something seems to be raised by a variety of respondents, for example).

2   *Inter-transcript analysis*: compare and contrast respondents. How is what they say alike? Different? Be prepared for more back-and-forth thinking (just like problem formulation) as you try to make meaning of respondents as a group, and stay open to the evolution of ideas, of themes, of meaning, etc.

> *All respondents talked about their early education. Some went to public school, some to private school. But they all talked about it as an important factor.*

In what terms? That's the question to answer now. Read over what they said; think about it; reread it; rethink it.

> *They all talked about its impact on their current attitudes toward authority.*

Okay, now you're beginning to get a collective story about the relationship between early education and adult reactions to authority from the group.

3   *Developing a story*: for your sample that includes all of the major themes you've noticed and including divergent cases and negative examples to round it out. The question to answer here is how this particular sample has answered your research question.

Major points to remember

- At the heart of qualitative analysis is some kind of content (spoken/written word) analysis.
- Analysis begins with clarity about the words and ends with interpretation.
- The concept of evidence is central to qualitative analysis.
- Qualitative analysis includes a "thick description" of every aspect of the study process.
- Some major issues to consider in qualitative analysis are audience, transferability, confirmability, saturation, completeness, range, divergence, and researcher bias.

Exercise

A touch of practice

1   Read a chapter in any book that particularly interests you, and then close it and put it away.
2   Take out paper and pencil (or the trusty word processor), and take a few pages to write about that chapter. Who is the author? What is the book about? What is the chapter about? What are the major points it tries to make?
3   Go back to that chapter. Now, for each major point that you identified, find an example in that chapter—phrases, sentences, paragraphs, etc. ("evidence")— that your identification of the major point/s is correct, on target.
4   Compare your notes with the chapter. Did you miss anything of importance? If not, then review your notes again; those major points ... should they be left as they are, or could/should you collapse them into categories (themes/points) at a greater level of abstraction? Should themes of education and parental discipline be collapsed into a broader category called childhood experiences, perhaps? Or would that then make them too broad?

No hard and fast rules. The name of the game is whatever makes for best representation of the material and best comprehension by the consumer of your work. Perhaps this is a good moment for a feedback session (going back to the source for confirmation of your own comprehension).

Reference

Glaser, B. G. and Strauss, A. L. (1967). *The Discovery of Grounded Theory: Strategies for Qualitative Research*. New York: Aldine de Gruyter.

22

QUANTITATIVE DATA ANALYSIS: MAKING SENSE OF DESCRIPTIVE STATS

(Yes, you can)

Key concepts

central tendency
description
distribution
frequency
generalization
index of dispersion
mean
median
mode
normal curve
range
standard deviation
typicality
variability/variation

Introduction

Descriptive stats are simply numbers that describe your quantitative findings in a visual nutshell through tables, charts, and graphs. Commonly associated with large-scale descriptive, experimental, and correlational studies, descriptive stats can also be found in other studies, however, if only to give an easy summary of certain sample characteristics or demographics, and in many mixed-method studies. Essentially, descriptive stats aim to summarize a sample, rather than use the data to learn about the population that the sample of data is thought to represent. Descriptive analysis can consist of *univariate* (looking at one variable only), *bivariate* analysis (looking at two variables together), and *multivariate* analysis (looking at several variables at once).

Some common ways to organize descriptive stats

There are many ways to organize descriptive stats; below are a few common ways.

Frequency tables

Frequency tables summarize how your sample responded for each variable on your instrument, including sample size, which can vary from item to item according to who did or didn't respond. Sometimes responses are referred to "valid" and nonresponses as "missing." Table 22.1 is an example.

TABLE 22.1 Example of a frequency table: age

	Age	*Frequency*	*Percent*	*Valid percent*	*Cumulative percent*
Valid	22	7	7.4	7.5	7.5
	23	11	11.6	11.8	19.4
	24	8	8.4	8.6	28.0
	25	9	9.5	9.7	37.6
	26	10	10.5	10.8	48.4
	27	12	12.6	12.9	61.3
	28	6	6.3	6.5	67.7
	29	3	3.2	3.2	71.0
	30	3	3.2	3.2	74.2
	31	5	5.3	5.4	79.6
	32	1	1.1	1.1	80.6
	33	1	1.1	1.1	81.7
	34	2	2.1	2.2	83.9
	36	2	2.1	2.2	86.0
	37	1	1.1	1.1	87.1
	38	3	3.2	3.2	90.3
	39	2	2.1	2.2	92.5
	42	1	1.1	1.1	93.5
	45	1	1.1	1.1	94.6
	47	1	1.1	1.1	95.7
	49	1	1.1	1.1	96.8
	51	1	1.1	1.1	97.8
	53	2	2.1	2.2	100.0
	Total	93	97.9	100.0	
Missing		2	2.1		
Total		95	100.0		

Note: N = 93; 2 missing; mean age 28.84; median age 27; mode age 27.

Frequency tables often include other basic descriptive stats, such as *central tendency* (the typical response for that question/item) and *variability* (how varied the individual responses are). Be sure to keep your visual representations both logical and organized. Table 22.2 organizes values from low (1/no responses in this example) to high (7); at a glance you see that the sample as a whole find life more rather than less stressful.

You can also describe in detail or grouped. Tables 22.3 and 22.4 illustrate the former and latter approaches, respectively.

How to decide? It depends on how much detail you want to offer. For example, for the purpose of your study do you really need to show each actual score (e.g., 50 subjects with a score each), or is grouping scores enough (e.g., 91–100, 81–90, 71–80, etc.)? You are the one to determine just how much detail your readers/consumers will need to understand your findings in context. (Often, be warned, it's less than you think; most people do not want [or are not interested in] the same amount of detail as the researcher.)

TABLE 22.2 Example of an ordinal low/high table: how stressful is your job?

	Stress value	Frequency	Percent	Valid percent	Cumulative percent
Not stressful	2	6	6.9	6.9	6.9
	3	2	2.3	2.3	9.2
	4	8	9.2	9.2	18.4
	5	36	41.4	41.4	59.8
	6	27	31.0	31.0	90.8
Very stressful	7	8	9.2	9.2	100.0
Total		87	100.0	100.0	100.0

Note: N = 87; 0 missing.

TABLE 22.3 Test scores

Score	Frequency	Percent	Cumulative percent
100	2	4	4
98	3	6	10
97	4	8	18
90	8	16	34
88	12	24	58
85	9	18	76
70	7	14	90
63	4	8	98
51	1	2	100
Total	50	100	100

Note: N = 50.

TABLE 22.4 Test scores

Score	Frequency	Percent	Cumulative percent
91–100	9	18	18
81–90	29	58	76
71–80	—	—	76
61–70	11	22	98
51–60	1	2	100
Total	50	100	100

Note: N = 50.

Pie charts

Pie charts are circular graphs with slices that total 100 percent. They're used to depict responses to nominal LOM variables. Figure 22.1 depicts one for respondents' religious preference in a sample of 100.

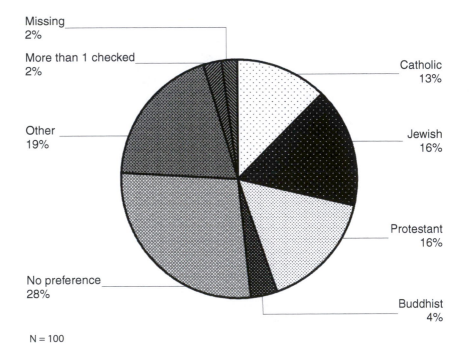

N = 100

FIGURE 22.1 Example of a pie chart: religious preference

Bar charts

Bar charts are commonly used to depict responses to ordinal LOM variables. The bars and spaces between them are of equal width. For example, Figure 22.2 depicts a bar chart for financial status, which was measured at the ordinal LOM in this particular study. In this sample most people's status falls in either the low or middle socioeconomic status ranks. Notice how easy it is to tell, at a quick glance, how the sample is distributed?

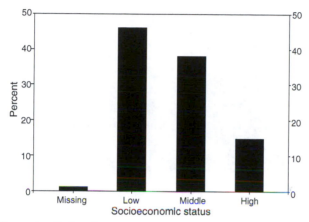

FIGURE 22.2 Example of a bar chart: socioeconomic status

Histograms

Histograms are like bar charts but commonly used to depict responses to interval or ratio LOM variables. Here, the bars touch to show mathematical continuity between the numbers. Figure 22.3 depicts age, a ratio LOM variable. Connecting

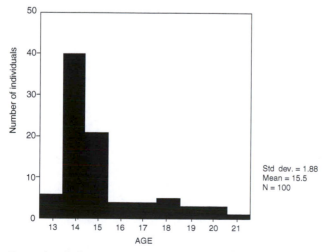

FIGURE 22.3 Example of a histogram: age

the tops of each bar by a line renders a kind of curve; and, depending on the sample's distribution (variation in how the responses fall), many curve shapes are possible. Figure 22.4 suggests a sample skewed toward the younger age group, revealing a *skewed* distribution.

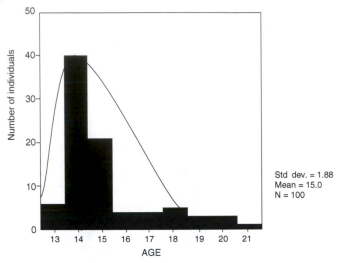

FIGURE 22.4 Example of a histogram showing skewed distribution of age

Contingency tables (aka crosstabs)

Contingency tables are commonly used to show association between two variables. Table 22.5 depicts association between gender within the sample and financial status.

Some contingency tables also include percentage figures in each cell under the absolute number.

TABLE 22.5 Example of a contingency table

	Financial status			
Gender	Overextended	Making ends meet	Comfortable	Total
Male	3	3	1	7
Female	37	30	12	79
Total	40	33	13	86

Note: N = 86.

Three rules of thumb in presenting visuals

1   Always give an overview of the distribution for your sample (give it a context so it doesn't just "appear" on the page).

2   Describe each visual to the reader (put into narrative what the figure says graphically; yes, it may seem redundant to you, but it will be helpful to the reader).
3   Make an interpretation (what the numbers imply). Be clear.

What else gets described?

For descriptive stats, along with the visuals you usually present *measures of central tendency* (stats that tell you what is typical for your sample) on any given variable or the instrument as a whole if it's interval or ratio LOM and *measures of variability* (stats that tell you about the nature and size of the variation of all the individual scores in your sample) on any given variable or the instrument as a whole if it's interval or ratio LOM (see Chapter 7).

• Central tendency is measured in three different ways: *mode, median,* and *mean* (average).
• Variability is measured in three different ways: *index of dispersion, range,* and *standard deviation.*

Think of central tendency as the forest and of variability as the trees; together, they give you a pretty good quantitative picture of your sample: what's "typical" about it along with the kind of variation within in.

Measures of central tendency

To speak of what's typical about your sample is to speak of *central tendency* (CT) Think about it. Central. Tendency. Typicality. As noted above, there are three ways to think about typicality of a sample in research (*mode, median, mean*), and it's important to know them, because each one is generally associated with a particular LOM and, as you'll see below, conceptualizes "typicality" in a slightly different way.

Mode

A *mode,* generally used to describe CT for *nominal* LOM variables, reflects the most frequent response category. Say the religious affiliation of your sample looks like this:

Orthodox	40%
Conservative	30%
Reform	20%
Unaffiliated	10%
Total	100%

You will note that the mode isn't necessarily a majority of the whole, just the most frequently responded-to (largest) category. Here, the Orthodox respondents aren't a majority, but their category is still the largest one, at 40 per cent.

The lens used to define CT in this case, then, seeks the largest category. Here's a trick for remembering what mode refers to. In French the word "mode" means vogue or fashion, like pie *à la mode*. So think about which category is "in vogue" (the one most in fashion)—that's the mode.

Median

A *median*, generally used to describe CT for *ordinal, interval, and ratio* LOM variables, reflects the middle-most point in your sample's distribution for any given quantitative variable. Say the distribution for number of years in practice for your sample of 20 social workers falls in the following way:

Sample member #: 1 2 3 4 5 6 7 8 9 10 11 12 13 14 15 16 17 18 19 20

Years in practice: 4 4 5 6 7 7 8 9 10 12 13 13 15 17 18 18 19 22 25 26

Here, the median (mid-most point) is 12.5 years. That is, half of the sample (ten people) has fewer than 12.5 years in practice and half of the sample (ten people) has more. In this case, then, the lens used to define CT seeks the number *above which* and *below which* half the cases fall. Think of the median strip in the highway. It's (theoretically, anyway) in the middle of the road, splitting the road into two equal halves.

Mean

With a *mean*, we become a little more sophisticated in looking at typicality, because a mean can become the basis for calculating inferential stats. A mean is like a mathematical average, and it's best used to describe CT for *interval* and *ratio* LOM variables. Based on real math, it's considered the most sophisticated CT measure. The mean is calculated by adding up all the numbers or "scores" in a distribution and dividing that sum by the number in that sample. To continue from the previous example, if there are:

20 members in the sample	20
and their sum total number of practice years	260
the mean (average) for this sample	260 divided by 20 = a mean of 13 (years in practice)

Sometimes the mean represents typicality quite well. Sometimes it doesn't. An extreme score, either high or low, can skew a distribution so much that the mean isn't really representative; if so, the mode or median are better (more accurate) measures to use.

Measures of variability

Measures of variability indicate the extent to which individual scores in any distribution (years in practice, ages, height, number of men in caseload, SAT scores, etc.) disperse—i.e., spread out—around their mean. Are all the other scores near the mean? Or do they vary widely, with some, for example, as low as 60 (with a mean of 80) and others, for example, as high as 99? This would mean there's an enormous variability in this sample. Some people scored as low as 60 and some as high as 99, while the mean (average) score was 80. On the other hand, if the lowest score was 75, for example, and the highest was 90, that would reflect much less variation in individual scores or, said differently, more test takers did alike. Say the mean score on a test taken by 25 people is 80. Okay, you know the "average" (mean) score for this distribution. But you don't know how widely individual scores vary around that mean. By knowing variability, you get a fuller picture of how they all did, not just the "average." Back we go to context … Knowing a bit about the whole picture, after understanding what's typical, gives us a better understanding of the full context.

Index of dispersion

Index of dispersion shows variability for *nominal* LOM variables by reflecting the percentage of cases that fall outside the mode. So if the mode is a category with 35 percent of the scores in it, the index of dispersion is .65. In this example, there's quite a bit of variation, because 65 percent of the sample is not reflected by the mode. If the mode is a category (remember, nominal LOM reflects categories) with 48 percent of the scores in it, on the other hand, with an index of dispersion is .52 (that percentage of the sample that falls outside of the mode), then you know that only 52 percent of the sample falls outside of the modal category, indicating less difference (variation) between the modal category and the rest of the response categories.

Range

The *range* shows variability for *ordinal*, *interval*, and *ratio* LOM variables and refers to the size of spread between a distribution's highest and lowest numbers. What's the lowest test score (or years in practice, or age, or weight) for your sample? And what's the highest? The difference between the two is the range (r).

Standard deviation

The *standard deviation (SD) stat (number)* shows variability for *interval* and *ratio* LOM variables and is calculated from the mean. It speaks to average distance of the individual scores from the mean. The greater that variability, the larger the SD stat.

Calculated how? Basically, probability theory says that in every naturally occurring phenomenon, a few cases always have much less of whatever attribute is being measured, a few always have much more of it, and that most cases cluster around the average (mean).

Think about your old school tests. Didn't a few people always do very poorly, a few always do really well, but most everyone do somewhere in the middle? That's a real-life example of this theory, which, in action, is called the *normal curve*. A visual rendition of this mathematical concept is shown in Figure 22.5.

What probability theory says, then, is that in any normal distribution (not too skewed by high or low scores):

1   about 68 percent of the scores will always fall within a specific distance to either side (+/−) of the mean called one standard deviation;
2   about 95 percent of them will always fall within a specific distance to either side (+/−) of the mean called two standard deviations; and
3   over 99 percent of them will always fall within a specific distance to either side (+/−) of the mean called three standard deviations.

So … picture yourself standing right on the top center of the normal curve depicted below. This puts you right on top where the mean, median, and mode meet. Now look as far as 1SD to each side; you should see about 68 percent of everyone's scores. Now look as far as 2SD to each side; you should see about 95 percent of them. And now look as far as 3SD to each side; you should see over 99 percent of them.

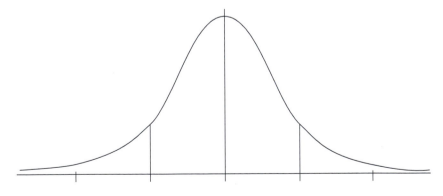

FIGURE 22.5 Example of a normal curve

Translated into the real world? Say a classroom of 25 students takes a test with a resulting mean score of 80 and an SD value of 5. For this distribution, then, each standard deviation unit is 5 points:

+1SD includes all scores as far up as 85
−1SD includes all scores as far down as 75
+2SD includes all scores as far up as 90
−2SD includes all scores as far down as 70
+3SD includes all scores as far up as 95
−3SD includes all scores as far down as 65.

Now, if you were to get back up on top of the mean for this particular distribution, which would put you at the number 80:

1   within 5 test score points to either side of you at 80 (the mean) (so, between 85 looking upward and 75 looking downward) or +/−1SD (since 1SD for this calculation equals 5 raw points) you would find about 68 percent of the class scores;

2   then, within 10 test score points to either side of you at 80 (the mean) (so, between 90 looking upward and 70 looking downward) or +/−2SD (since 1SD for this calculation equals 5 raw points) you would find about 95 percent of the class scores;

3   finally, within 15 test score points to either side of you, at 80 (the mean) (so, between 95 looking upward and 65 looking downward) or +/−3SD (since 1SD for this calculation equals 5 raw points) you would find just about all the scores (about 99 percent).

As you can see, in this sample there's quite a bit of variation; some test scores are as high as 95, while others are as low as 65!

If, for example, the mean were 80 with an SD value of 2:

1   you'd find about 68 percent of the test scores between a lowest score (or scores) of 78 and highest of 82 (+/−1SD or 2 raw points in either direction of the mean);

2   you'd find about 95 percent of the test scores between a lowest score (or scores) of 76 and highest of 84 (+/−2SD or 4 raw points in either direction)

3   and you'd find over 99 percent of the test scores between a lowest score (or scores) of 74 and highest of 86 (+/−3SD or 6 raw points in either direction).

In this example, that the individual scores would be hovering more closely to one another around the mean indicates that test takers scored pretty closely to one another and thus the whole picture reflects less variability.

Why should you care?

Well, for one thing, as noted above it's useful to know just how well the mean actually represents the sample. The larger the standard deviation value, the greater the variability, meaning that individual scores tend to differ from the mean.

Second, measures of variability provide a language for comparing numbers when they're used differently. Say you give a group of people two tests: a self-esteem measure that scores from 70 to 100 and an eating-habits test that scores from 1 to 10. Group A's mean score is 85 on the self-esteem test and 6 on the eating-habits test. How can you compare the scores? You can't. Or say Mrs. Smith got an 85 on the self-esteem test and 7 on the eating-habits test. How can you compare 85 and 7? You can't. The numbers are used so differently it's the old apples and oranges problem. Yet, it's this very kind of comparison that social work is often very interested. What to do?

So now we translate the values (actual scores) into standard units that reflect deviation (variation) from the mean (from any mean), just like the examples above, and voilà! We have a language (referred to as z scores) that now provides a common denominator for comparing apples and oranges (you might say that z scores are a way of translating apples and oranges into the common denominator of "fruit!").

Major points to remember

*   Statistics are numbers, used in various ways to summarize your quantitative findings and often presented in visual nutshells through tables, charts, and graphs.
*   Descriptive analysis consists of *univariate* analysis, *bivariate* analysis, and *multivariate* analysis.
*   Three measure of *central tendency* describe what's typical for your sample: *mode* (the most frequent response category), *median* (the middle-most point in the distribution for your sample), and *mean* (basically, the average for your sample).
*   Three measures of *variability* describe variation within your sample: *index of dispersion* (how individual responses distribute around the sample's mean), *range* (the distance between lowest "score" response and highest), and *standard deviation* (how individual scores, on average, vary around the sample's mean).

Exercise

Now what?

1   Match the description to the visual:

_____ circular graph	A Bar chart
_____ bars touch one another	B Histogram
_____ bars do not touch one another	C Pie chart

2   Match the description to the visual:
      _____ commonly used to depict nominal LOM variables   A   Bar chart
      _____ commonly used to depict ordinal LOM variables   B   Histogram
      _____ commonly used to depict interval/ratio LOM variables C   Pie chart

		True	false?
3	You've got ordinal LOM data. The *mean* will be a good measure of central tendency.	____	____
4	You've got interval LOM data. *Index of dispersion* will be a good measure of central tendency.	____	____
5	The *mode* reflects the middle-most point in a distribution.	____	____
6	You've got nominal LOM data. The *median* will be a good measure of variability.	____	____
7	*Index of dispersion* is a good measure of typicality.	____	____
8	You've got interval LOM data. The *range* is a possible measure of variability.	____	____
9	The larger the variation of individual scores in a distribution, the larger the SD stat.	____	____
10	The *mean*, *median*, and *mode* of a normal curve always coincide.	____	____

23

QUANTITATIVE DATA ANALYSIS: MAKING SENSE OF INFERENTIAL STATS

(Yes, you can ... really!)

Key concepts

confidence
correlation
difference
directionality
inference
probability
sample error
statistical power
statistical significance

Introduction

Inferential stats tell you:

1 if difference or association is significant (real/true/accurate) within your sample or probably due to chance or some error in sampling; and
2 if you can infer that the look (characteristics) of the population resembles the look (characteristics) of the sample and thus with what level of confidence you can generalize from your sample to its population.

Remember we're talking here about quantitative data (inherently numerical or numerically coded in some way) in probability samples.

How to use inferential stats

To use inferential stats means to carry out certain mathematical computations (now carried out by many computer programs, such as SPSS) called tests of statistical significance. There are many such tests. They're all based on your descriptive stats but use different ones in different ways. They all use different mathematical calculations, and the one you use depends on the LOM of the variable/s in question. But, again, what they all do is answer these questions:

1   *Can I infer that a difference or association noted in this sample is significant, or is it probably just a chance thing or due to sampling error?*
2   *Can I infer that the look of my population resembles the look of my sample enough to confidently generalize whatever I find of significance for the sample to that population?*

Say you give a standardized test on verbal skills to two randomly assigned groups of children. Experimental group scores range from 50 to 75, with a of mean (average) of 60. Comparison group scores range from 52 to 76, with a mean (average) of 60. Okay, you have a few descriptive stats for each group: lowest/highest scores, range, and mean. Then, you conduct a skills-building program for the experimental group and to each member of the comparison group you give a skills-building book to read on their own. Your skills-building program intervention ends, and you test everyone again—both groups.

Post-test scores for the experimental group range from a low score of 55 (up 5 points from the pre-test) to a high score of 85 (up 10 points from the pre-test) with a mean score of 70 (up 10 points from the pre-test). *Great*, you think to yourself. Things look good for your intervention! It looks like your program did its job: it increased the skillsets of the group that participated (the experimental group).

Now you look at the post-test scores of the comparison group (the group that received the self-help books).

Post-test scores for the comparison group range from a low score of 55 (so, up 3 points from the pre-test) to a high score of 82 (up 6 points from the pre-test) with a mean score of 65 (up 5 points from the pre-test). Huh! They did better too! *Huh?* Here's the thing. Your experimental group had higher scores at the end of your program, but so did the comparison group (not an unrealistic scenario). Now what? How do you know if the difference you think you see between them is significant (far away enough from what chance would have dictated anyway) that the experimental group did better as a result of your program, especially now that they *both* did better? You don't. But if you subject your descriptive stats to significance testing, you can find out.

Using probability theory to calculate mathematical relationships between or among descriptive stats, *significance tests* let you: (1) infer whether or not a difference (or correlation) is in fact significant (that is, greater than that which chance alone would have dictated); and, if so, (2) with just what level of confidence you can generalize that difference or correlation to the sample's population—just how likely what you find in your sample "holds water" for its parent population as well.

Since inference by any other name always denotes uncertainty, however, probability theory is integral to inferential stats. Basically, probability theory says that it is more likely than not that what you find is *not* significant. The job of inferential stats, then, is to evaluate the odds of making a mistake if you do make a claim that differences or associations are significant. Here's a bit more of what you need to know about probability.

Three related laws of probability

Three important laws of probability (paraphrased here) govern and guide the calculation of inferential stats:

1   No matter how good your random sampling strategy, and even if a stat test suggests that a finding is significant (a real/true/accurate group difference or correlation), you still must acknowledge at least one chance of being incorrect due to an unknown but possible bias in your sample (sample error).

This "humanity factor" is acknowledged as *margin of error* (or minimum sample error) and is calculated from standard deviation (units you learned about in the preceding chapter, now called *standard error units*; same thing, different name). Clearly, the smaller the better (as with any "error"). What does it mean, practically speaking in plain English? Your random sample better be truly random. Cheating makes all your findings meaningless!

2   Don't worry that random sampling ten times in one population is likely to get you ten somewhat different samples (i.e., ten random-number tables to select a sample of 100 out of a sample frame of 1,000 would get you ten different final samples), because over the long run (many, many samples)—as long as those samples have integrity (are truly random)—their distributions tend to look very alike. In short, a few samples from the same frame might look different, but over a long haul, the differences even out, and they end up looking more alike than not. This law is called the central limit theorem (CLT).

Thus, no matter which of many possible samples from a population you end up with, if your sampling method was truly random you can have a 95 percent confidence level (95 percent probability) that the average population score for any distribution will be within $+/-2$ standard error units of your sample's average score.

Huh? Okay, remember standing right in the middle (on the mean) of the top of the normal curve and looking to either side as far as 1SD, 2SD, and 3SD to see how individual scores varied from the average score for that sample's distribution? Get back up there. Now look only as far as two of those units to either side. The CLT says that whatever the mean is for your sample (unless it's got only 30 members or fewer or is badly skewed), you have a 95 percent chance that somewhere within that four-unit space (two to your left, two to your right) you will find the average score for your population (that larger group from whence you drew your sample).

Why should you care? Because this 95 percent confidence level has been established in social science as the minimum level for claiming significance of any kind and is factored into the math calculation of all stat tests. In other words, social science convention says that you can only claim significance and generalizability of your findings (what you found for your sample) if a statistical test (devoted to this kind of analysis) says you have a 95 percent or better chance of being correct (indicated by the p value at the end of every test).

The upshot? The upshot is this. If the results of the test indicate that you have only a 94 percent chance (shown as p .06) of being correct (and thus, a 6 percent chance of being *incorrect*), forget about claiming significance or generalizability. If stat test results indicate that you have a 95 percent (p .05) chance of being correct (and thus, a 5 percent chance of being incorrect should you claim significance or generalizability of your findings), clap your hands! And if the test shoots out p .02, then it is saying that you have a 98 percent chance of being correct (and thus only a 2 percent chance of being incorrect) if you claim significance or generalizability, so jump for joy!

3   The larger your sample the more likely its mean will resemble the mean of the population from whence you drew that sample. This is called the law of large numbers. Makes sense, right? Thus, a random sample of 50 has more chances to resemble its population of 100 than a random sample of ten. So if you are interested in large populations and plan on random sampling in order to be able to generalize what you find out about your final sample to that population, remember that the larger the sample the better.

The testing process

All inferential stats are based on testing either a hypothesis of group difference or a hypothesis of association (correlation), each of which can be formulated at a broad level:

Example: Formulation of group difference

> *There's a significant difference in how Group A and Group B scored overall on this instrument* or, at a more detailed level, *There's a significant difference in how Group A and Group B scored on Item #5 on this questionnaire.*

Example: Formulation of association

> *There's a significant association between the overall scores on Measure A (one instrument) and Measure B (another instrument) for this one group* or, at a more

detailed level, *There's a significant association between the overall scores on Item #4 (one variable) and Item #6 (another variable) for this one group.*

Hypotheses of group difference

Example: Comparing differences between two on one variable.

You wonder: *Is there a significant difference between Group A and Group B on this variable?*

In order to engage in statistical testing to find this out, you formulate a hypothesis, which is step one of statistical testing.

You hypothesize: *There is a significant difference between Group A and Group B.*

You state your hypothesis in the positive (there *is* a difference), because hypotheses are generally stated in the positive direction, with the null version of the hypothesis stated in the negative.

And then you formulate a null version of that hypothesis, which is what you will subject to statistical testing to find out if your hypothesis "holds water" (remember?):

> *No siree (says the Null Hypothesis), there's no significant difference between the groups! Now go ahead and prove me wrong!*

So you subject that null version of your hypothesis to the appropriate stat test, (that is, you ask a statistical software program to carry out a certain test), and you check the results. If the test (calculation) indicates that you should reject your null hypothesis with a 95 percent confidence level, you can substantiate your hypothesis (yea!).

The two types of groups for which we test difference are:

1   *independent sample groups* (most random samples); and
2   *correlated sample groups* (longitudinal samples in which your pre-intervention and post-intervention samples are conceptualized as two different groups [even with the same members], and *matching groups* in which some members are in the sample only because of their relationship to other members [husbands of wives, siblings of siblings, clients of workers, etc.]).

Why distinguish between groups? Because the stat tests for each type use slightly different mathematics. Also, independent-group testing is usually interested in raw scores as well comparison (so incorporates more calculations), while correlated-group testing is primarily interested in comparison (as in how husbands and wives compare on a marital satisfaction test rather than how they do in absolute terms) and so seeks fewer stats.

Comparing differences between more than two groups around more than one variable is of course possible but takes you into the world of more advanced statistics.

Hypotheses of association

Example: Examining potential association in one group around two or more variables.

You look over the results of a questionnaire distributed to a large number of people. Based on the purpose of your study, you begin to wonder about the responses to two items (age and income) in particular.

You wonder: *Is there a significant correlation between Variable 1 (e.g., age) and Variable 2 (e.g., income) for this sample?*

In order to engage in statistical testing to find this out, you formulate a hypothesis, which is here again step one of statistical testing.

You hypothesize: *There is a significant correlation between age and income for this sample.*

And then you formulate a null version:

No siree, there's no significant correlation between age and income in this sample!

You then subject this null version to a stat test (that is, you ask a statistical software program to carry out a certain test), and you check the results. If the test says to reject your null hypothesis with a 95 percent confidence level, you can substantiate your original hypothesis (yea!).

Directionality

Oh yes … one more thing to consider. Whether you want to test difference or association, the hypothesis can be stated in either *directional* or *nondirectional* terms.

Group difference

Directional hypothesis: *Women keep their appointments at the clinic more often than men.*

Nondirectional hypothesis: *There's a significant difference between men and women in keeping appointments at the clinic.*

Association

Directional hypothesis: *Attitude toward service affects level of participation.*

Nondirectional hypothesis: *Attitude (Variable 1) and level of participation (Variable 2) are associated.*

You can see that a *directional* version predicts the nature of difference (women [Group 1] keep their appointments more frequently than men [Group 2]) or association (attitude [Variable 1] has an impact on level of participation [Variable 2], not vice versa); while a *nondirectional* version proposes a difference or association without predicting its nature. In the case of group difference, it proposes that there is a difference between the genders (but who knows what that difference is). In the case of association, it proposes that attitude and participation are related, but who knows which affects the other (which comes first, in other words).

Here's an important rule of thumb: if you think you're "intelligent" enough to predict the nature of a difference (*not only is there a difference, but here's what I think it is*) or association (*not only are these two variables related, but here's how I think they are related*), go ahead and formulate a directional version of your hypothesis, and test it by subjecting its null version to a statistical test.

But here's the catch: if the stat test results indicates that, in fact, it's the opposite of what you predicted, too bad! For example, if men keep their appointments equal to women or more so, then you must refute your hypothesis, and that's that. Or if you hypothesize that attitude affects participation and the test suggests that, in fact, participation seems to affect attitude, then again, you must refute your hypothesis. If you want to play it safe, therefore, by not predicting the nature of the difference or association, formulate a nondirectional hypothesis, and go ahead and test its null version. Then, if whatever difference or association is indicated as true/real/accurate by your testing process, you can substantiate your hypothesis. Perhaps women do better than men. Or perhaps men do better than men. Perhaps attitude seems to affect participation. Or perhaps participation seems to affect attitude. Whatever the case, you did not specify direction of difference or association, so your hypothesis is good to go. Yeah!

In a nutshell

To test statistical significance of any quantitative finding:

1   You transform your question of interest into a hypothesis of group difference or association, either directional or nondirectional. (How bold are you? Think about the purpose of your study, and if it makes sense with that purpose and you feel bold, go for direction. If not, don't.)

2   You transform that hypothesis into its null version (not the opposite, just stating that what you are hypothesizing isn't so).

3 You subject that null hypothesis to a stat test that has been created to test either difference or association based on the LOM of your variables.
4 If and only if that test rejects your null hypothesis with a 95 percent or higher confidence level can you accept your original hypothesis.

Significance testing: possibilities for error

The math involved in stat testing has been developed and refined over a long period of time and with great care. However, there are still errors that these tests might make:

1 *Type I error (aka A/alpha)*: the statistical test to which you subjected your null hypothesis says it's okay to accept your hypothesis (reject the null) when really, if truth were known, you should refute it. Uh oh! Here you go, claiming significance or association when there really isn't any!
2 *Type II error (aka B/beta)*: the statistical test to which you subjected your null hypothesis tells you to reject your hypothesis (accept the null) when really, if truth were known, you should accept it. Oh, dear! Here you go, crying over no significance or association when really there is one!
3 *Type III error*: Unfortunately, you are way past the moment when you should have given this some thought. Here you are, having collected data from a random sample, and you are now in full analysis ... but the problem is, if truth were known, you asked the wrong question! In this case, the misstep was in your problem identification process. You concluded that a certain question needed asking, and then you went about the proper research methodology to answer it. Unfortunately, however, you asked the wrong question. Now that you have got to the point of statistical testing, what has happened is that your false null hypothesis *is* rejected (that's a good thing, in effect, because it means your original hypothesis can be accepted), *but* the claimed truth inherent in your hypothesis is actually the opposite of what it really is (truth be known).

How to prevent such catastrophes?

1 Integrity of sampling method is essential—so don't cheat! But also, say your final sample is only 80 questionnaires out of 150 sent out. Uh oh. That's a pretty big difference. How do you know some special bias hasn't crept into that final sample? What to do? Pay attention to these possibilities up front.
2 Using the right stat test for the right variable LOM is important. Using the incorrect test can yield incorrect results.
3 Think about the potential for a Type III error as you educate yourself about your area of inquiry. Check and recheck with as many experts on the subject as you can so that you become as certain as possible to ask the right question. You can see that the entire validity of your study is in question here should you be asking the wrong question! Imagine feeling self-satisfied enough with

the results of your study (after all that time and work) and publishing the results only to have someone call you up and say, *Oh dear, you know what? I think you asked the wrong question to begin with!*

How mathematically sensitive a test is to reduce the potential for making either of the first two possible errors is referred to as its statistical power. The group of tests (called parametric tests) that examine difference/association at the interval/ratio LOM are much more powerful than those (nonparametric tests) that examine difference/association at the nominal/ordinal LOM because they use numbers in a real way (unlike numbers used to code categorical [nominal] or ordinal data, for example).

The more powerful tests are based on certain assumptions about the sample and should be used only when those assumptions are met in reality. Because they've shown themselves to be such good indicators of significance even when the assumptions are not fully met, however, they often get used at the nominal/ordinal LOM as well. They really shouldn't.

How to know the probability of making these errors? Look for the p value at the end of every stat test. It tells you the probability (p = probability) that a Type I or Type II error will have been made if you substantiate your hypothesis that the difference/association you tested is significant. Thus, p .04 means if you claim significance you have four chances in 100 (4 percent) according to that test of being incorrect (making a Type I or Type II error); p .11 says you have 11 chances in 100 (11 percent) of being incorrect. And p .001 says you have one chance in 1,000 of being incorrect.

Mmm ... one chance in 1,000 of being incorrect ... That seems quite acceptable. Four chances in 100? Not too bad. But 11 in 100? Now that's scary! Would you be willing to make this claim, say, in all the newspapers of the world?

> *According to my research, there's a significant difference in intelligence between the genders. ... Of course, the statistical testing process indicates that I have 11 chances in 100 of being wrong on this, but I'm willing to accept those odds.*

What do you think? Could you take that risk? Social science convention won't. The social science research convention is to claim significance only if p (probability of being mistaken) is .05 or smaller. Basically, it says this:

> *Look, if the test says I have five chances or fewer in 100 of being mistaken in claiming significance, that's not bad; I can live with those odds.*

So for social science research p .05 is acceptable. But that's the limit; p .06 is not acceptable. And no, it's not *almost* acceptable. It's about as "acceptable" as being "a little bit" pregnant. Of course, different sciences have different conventions, and even within them the conventions vary according to the consequences of being mistaken. For example, p .01, which is excellent for social science, may not be acceptable to medical research, which often requires a much greater confidence level, such as p .001—that is, one chance in 1,000 of being in error in making claims around the likelihood of a new drug causing birth defects, for example.

Statistical significance versus meaning

Statistical significance and meaning. How do they relate to each other? Remember that statistical significance is the result of a mathematical calculation that indicates the probability of a difference or association between your quantitative findings being a real/true/accurate representation or just a chance thing or due to some error in your research process:

> Yes, the difference/association you're testing is probably real/true/accurate, and here are the odds that you'll be mistaken if you say so.

> No, the difference/association you're testing is probably not real/true/ accurate.

> And yes, what you see and find in your sample probably also holds water for its parent population.

> No, what you see and find in your sample probably doesn't hold water for its population.

But now, you need to make meaning of the results. You need to return to the idea of *context*. What does significance or lack thereof suggest given the purpose of your study? What can be learned from the results within the context of your study? What questions can be answered? What new ones are raised? You've described your findings; now interpret them within the context of your study first and then in context of your research topic and what others have found. That's how you make meaning of your statistical findings and use them to add to the existing body of knowledge. Significance testing is a means to an end, then, not an end in and of itself. It is useful toward intra–sample meaning of quantitative data (what you can infer from the results for the sample itself) and extra-sample meaning (what you can infer to and thus know about the population of interest from whence you drew that sample). Only when statistical significance is considered, analyzed, and presented in real-world terms (context) does it take on meaning.

Major points to remember

- Inferential stats are numbers that tell you if your findings are significant for your sample and how confidently you can generalize them to the population.
- Inferential stats are based on descriptive stats.
- To produce inferential stats is to carry out tests of statistical significance.

- Statistical significance tests use different descriptive stats and different mathematics, depending on the LOM of the variable/s to be tested.
- Inferential stats are guided by three laws of probability about (1) potential for sample error, (2) resemblance of random samples in a population, and (3) sample size.
- Tests of statistical significance test hypotheses of group difference or hypotheses of association.
- Each type of hypothesis has a directional and nondirectional version, each of which requires its own particular statistical test version.
- Three types of errors can be made in testing inference: Type I error occurs when a test rejects a null hypothesis by mistake; Type II error occurs when a test accepts a null hypothesis by mistake; and Type III error occurs when you have asked the wrong question to begin with.
- Integrity of sample and using appropriate tests can help to prevent the first two types of errors. Only becoming very well informed about your area of inquiry can help to prevent the third type.
- The mathematical sensitivity of a test to reduce the potential for making either of the first two types of error is referred to as its statistical power.
- p values indicate the probability of making a Type I or Type II error if significance is claimed.
- Social science research convention is to accept significance at p .05 or higher confidence level. This reflects a 95 percent confidence level in the accuracy of your findings.

Exercise

Test yourself

		True	False
1	You only need to use statistical significance tests if you can't tell significance from eyeballing the data.	_____	_____
2	Inferential stats only apply to experimental and correlational designs.	_____	_____
3	A 95 percent confidence level means that if a test indicates significant difference or association and you make that claim, you have five chances in 100 of still being incorrect.	_____	_____
4	Directionality applies only to hypotheses of group difference.	_____	_____
5	p .04 means you have six chances in 100 of making an incorrect claim of significance about your hypothesis.	_____	_____
6	Inferential stats help you determine the degree to which you can safely generalize from a sample to a population.	_____	_____

7   Size of sample doesn't matter when working with
    inferential stats as long as you used some kind of
    random sampling method to obtain it.   _____   _____
8   Statistical power refers to the credibility of quantitative
    data.   _____   _____
9   You've carried out your study. You've found 30
    people to interview, and you've transcribed and
    numerically coded their narratives. Now that you've
    got them coded, which of these inferential processes
    can you use?
    •   You can develop a hypothesis of difference based
        on what you've learned about your sample and
        subject it to testing for significance.   _____   _____
    •   You can develop a hypothesis of association based
        on what you've learned about your sample and
        subject it to testing for significance.   _____   _____
    •   You can use the codes to calculate central
        tendency and subject those stats to inference testing. _____   _____

Answers

Answers: (1) False; (2) False; (3) True; (4) False (it applies to hypotheses of association as well); (5) False
(4 chances out of 100); (6) True; (7) False; (8) False; (9) None! (no random sampling involved, and
qualitative data codes aren't used as a basis for descriptive or inferential stats).

24

TESTS OF STATISTICAL SIGNIFICANCE

(Getting confident!)

Key concepts

association
confidence level
correlated samples
correlation coefficient
critical value
group difference
independent samples
level of measure
one-tailed test
probability
statistical significance
test value
two-tailed test

How they work

All statistical significance tests yield a statistic (number); for example, a t test yields a t stat, an F test an F stat, a chi-square test a chi-square stat, etc. That stat is referred to as the *test value*, and, with the exception of one type of test, it can range from 1 to 3, based on the three standard error units (known by descriptive stats as standard deviation units) to either side of the mean in a distribution of scores.

Probability theory (always thumbing its nose!) says that our chances of finding significant difference or association are zero (nil, none, nada), remember? So, the farther away from zero the test value (stat), then, the more likely that any significance noted by the test's mathematical calculations is real/true/accurate. While a test value (except for one type of test) might range from 1 to 3, then, the point at which it begins to reflect significance, known as its *critical value*, is 1.96.

So the calculation of any (except for one) statistical test must yield a test value of 1.96 or greater for you to claim that a difference or association noted by that test is, in fact, significant. In this case, then, bigger is better!

Choosing a test

This is how you make sure to select the correct statistical test for what you want to test (group difference or association, directional or not, LOM of the variable/s in question, etc.):

1   You choose to enter one of two "families" of tests: the one that tests for significance of group difference or the one that tests for significance of association (correlation). Remember these from the previous chapter?
2   You then select the test that's correct for the level of measure (LOM) at which the variable/s in question have been measured (nominal, ordinal, interval, or ratio). For tests of group difference, you select tests appropriate for testing either independent sample groups or correlated sample groups.
3   You then go to the directional or nondirectional version of that test, depending on how you formulated your hypothesis to be tested:
  •   The directional version, called *one-tailed*, only looks in the distribution's (curve's) tails that can confirm or refute the direction of your hypothesis; it doesn't tell you if the opposite of your hypothesis is true, for example.
  •   The nondirectional version, called *two-tailed*, is a kinder, gentler version. Not as picky as its directional counterpart, it looks throughout the distribution (curve) to see if there's any difference or association whatsoever (a nondirectional hypothesis is willing to take any difference or association it can get, remember?).
4   You subject your descriptive stats to testing as called for by that particular test, and you examine the results primarily for two things: (1) the test stat (value), and (2) the confidence level (p).

A few common tests of group difference

Chi-square test

The *chi-square* test of statistical significance generally tests independent sample differences between two or more groups on *nominal* LOM data or when distribution is very skewed. Chi-square is a very common test in social work research, because so many data of interest are measured at the nominal LOM.

The math in this test calculates the difference between your findings (*observed frequency*) and what probability would normally dictate (*expected frequency*). If the chi-square stat (value) that the test yields is significant at p .05 or higher confidence level, you can substantiate your hypothesis that a significant difference exists between the groups. Calculated on the actual number of cases in the groups rather than their means (because the mean does not pertain to nominal variables), a chi-square stat (value) is always much larger than those of other tests.

Fisher Exact is used instead for two groups of small independent samples (30 or fewer). *McNemar Change* and *Cochran Q* examine correlated sample differences between two and two or more groups, respectively, on nominal LOM data.

Mann-Whitney U test

The *Mann-Whitney U* test of statistical significance tests independent sample differences between two groups on *ordinal* LOM data. Since numbers have no inherent value here except as codes, the test math rank orders the members of each group and then compares either their actual or averaged ranks. If the U stat (value) is 1.96 or larger at p .05 or higher confidence level, you can substantiate your hypothesis that a significant difference exists between the groups.

Kruskal-Wallis tests independent sample differences between two or more groups. *Wilcoxon t* and *Friedman Anova* (Anova = analysis of variance) test correlated sample difference between two and two or more groups, respectively, on ordinal LOM data.

t tests

An independent t test examines independent sample differences between two groups on *interval* or *ratio* LOM data by comparing the differences in their means. Here, finally, at the interval or ratio level of measure, we are dealing with numbers of real value even if the variable cannot logically be quantified, such as depression, at least one can say that one person scored twice as high as another on the depression test (although we cannot say, of course, that the former is twice as depressed). If the t stat (value) is yielded by the math calculation is 1.96 or larger at p .05 or higher confidence level, you can substantiate your hypothesis that there's a significant difference between the groups.

Say you give a scholastic aptitude test to two groups. You then calculate the mean of each. Group A has a mean of 800; Group B has a mean of 750. Is that a significant difference between them? We don't know. But through certain math calculations based on their means and variance (how much the individual scores vary from the mean), a t test tells you if it probably is or isn't. If the test says it is, then it is. But like pregnancy, difference isn't a little or kind of or almost significant. It is, or it isn't.

Anova (aka *F test*) examines independent sample differences between two or more groups. *Correlated t* and *correlated samples F test* examine correlated sample differences between two and two or more groups, respectively, on interval or ratio LOM.

A few common tests of association

To examine correlation is to look at the nature of a relationship between variables (not cause and effect but if they have a meaningful relationship), such as possible correlation between culture and attitude, or incarceration and recidivism, or personal history and present behavior, or gender and experience, etc. And just as tests of difference are based on the LOM of the variables in question, so are tests of association.

Phi coefficient

Phi coefficient tests for association when each variable has only two categories (such as Variable 1 with *male* or *female* response options and Variable 2 with *yes* or *no* response options).

Contingency coefficient

Contingency coefficient tests for association when the variables have equal but more than two categories (such as Variable 1 with three response options of *Muslim, Jewish,* or *Christian* and Variable 2 with response options of *under 30 years old, 30 to 50 years old,* or *over 50 years old*).

Spearman's Rho

Spearman's Rho tests for association between ordinal LOM variables by comparing ranks on each variable. Although Spearman's Rho is the technically correct test to use, *Pearson's r*, intended to measure association for interval or ratio LOM variables, has been proven to be so good at measuring ordinal LOM data as well that it's often used instead. Spearman's Rho is also used when assumptions necessary for Pearson's r (the more powerful test) cannot be met and the researcher's paying attention to that fact!

Pearson's r

Pearson's r tests for association between interval or ratio LOM variables by comparing the means on each variable, and they yield an r stat (value) commonly referred to as a *correlation coefficient.* Uh oh! You want to examine association between two variables with different LOMs? No problem.

Just use whichever test is appropriate for the variable with the lower LOM.

Talking about correlation

A correlation coefficient ("cc") can range from weak to strong (within a range of 0 to 1) and be either positive (+) or negative (−). Thus, a correlation might be weak or moderate or strong in either positive or negative territory.

A positive correlation is when the variables co-vary in the same direction ("more" of one variable is found, whatever it reflects, with "more" of the other, whatever it reflects). Higher self-esteem with higher education? Positive correlation. Lower self-esteem with lower education? Positive correlation.

A negative correlation is when the variables co-vary in opposite directions ("more" presence of one variable, whatever it reflects, with "less" presence of the other, whatever it reflects). Higher incidence of attention-seeking behaviors with lower self-esteem? Negative correlation.

Here's the scale for assessing strength and direction:

−1.00 = perfect negative correlation
− .95 = strong negative correlation
− .50 = moderate negative correlation
− .10 = weak negative correlation
  .00 = no correlation at all
+ .10 = weak positive correlation
+ .50 = moderate positive correlation
+ .95 = strong positive correlation
+1.00 = perfect positive correlation (e.g., something correlated with itself)

Here too, however, note that the p value at the end of the test must be p .05 or higher to substantiate your hypothesis of association.

Degrees of freedom

Most statistical tests factor into their calculations the amount of variation that must occur around the mean (or ranks or actual cell count) of the distribution of each group being compared before their difference is probably not significant. A *degrees of freedom* (df) stat is generally presented as a real number (1, 2, 6, etc.), and, usually, the larger the sample the smaller it is. The statistical test considers either (1) the number of groups being compared or (2) the number of people (cases) in each sample or (3) both, and it calculates the degrees of freedom that must be incorporated into the math.

Multivariate analysis

Multivariate testing refers to tests of statistical significance that examine several groups around several variables and several variables around several groups. There are many such tests, and they can be quite complex. With those, you begin to move into the world of advanced stats.

Major points to remember

- All statistical significance tests yield a statistic, referred to as their test value.
- The larger the test value, the more likely that any significance noted by the test's math is real/true/accurate.
- Selecting a proper test of statistical significance includes choosing (1) one of difference or association; (2) one that is appropriate for the LOM of the data in question (and for tests of difference, (3) the version that is appropriate to either independent or correlated sample groups); and (4) either a one-tailed or two-tailed test version, depending on nature of hypothesis.
- A few common tests of group difference are chi-square, Fisher Exact, McNemar Change, Cochran Q for nominal LOM data; Mann-Whitney U, Kruskal-Wallis, Wilcoxon t, and Friedman Anova for ordinal LOM data; and independent t, Anova/F test, correlated t, and correlated samples F test for interval and ratio LOM data.
- A few common tests of association are Phi coefficient, Contingency coefficient, Spearman's Rho, and Pearson's r.
- To examine association between two variables that have different levels of measure (LOM), you must use the test appropriate to the lower LOM.
- Correlation coefficients ("cc")—the stats that result from testing for association—range from weak to strong (from 0 to 1) and can be either positive or negative.
- Degrees of freedom ("df") speak to the amount of variation that can occur in each distribution being compared before a difference or association is determined as probably not significant. A df stat is factored into the calculations of most statistical tests.
- Degrees of freedom are calculated from either the number of groups being compared or number of people (cases) in each sample or both.

Exercise

Test yourself

1   For all but one statistical significance test, the test stat (value) can range from:

       _____ a   1 to 3

       _____ b   1 to 4

       _____ c   2 to 3

2 The closer to zero the test stat (value), the more probable that any significance noted by the test's math is real/true/accurate. True or false? (Circle your answer.)

3 The critical value of most tests is:

_____ a   .96

_____ b   1.96

_____ c   2.96

4 A positive correlation coefficient is said to be strong, and a negative one is said to be weak. True or false?

5 +1.00 and −1.00 are both perfect correlations. True or false?

6 Match the test to the data to be tested.

   Test:
   A   Chi-square
   B   Contingency coefficient
   C   Mann-Whitney U
   D   Pearson's r
   E   Phi coefficient
   F   Spearman's Rho
   G   t test

   Data to be tested:

   _____ group difference for nominal LOM data

   _____ group difference for ordinal LOM data

   _____ group difference for interval/ratio LOM data

   _____ association between nominal LOM variables with two categories each

   _____ association between nominal LOM variables with more than three but an equal number of categories each

   _____ association between ordinal LOM variables

   _____ association between interval or ratio LOM variables

7 You decide to carry out a longitudinal study of the impact of a special group program for teenagers on conflict resolution skills. You are able to random-select a sample of 20 to participate in your group, which will take place once a week for ten weeks. Before the program begins, you give each sample member a *Conflict Resolution Skills Test* to test them on their current skill level.

You carry out your program, test them again with the same instrument, and test them again every six months for the next two years. These two groups are:

_____ independent samples

_____ correlated samples

For whichever you select, why?

8   With this same longitudinal study, you then decide to see if at the last post-test there are any differences between the males and females in the sample around overall skill level as measured by the test. You are testing a hypothesis of:

_____ group difference

_____ association

For whichever you select, why?

9   You decide that girls probably have a higher skill level than boys. Therefore you formulate your hypothesis as:

_____ directional

_____ nondirectional

For whichever you select, why?

10   The test of statistical significance you then subject your hypothesis is a:

_____ one-tailed version

_____ two-tailed version

For whichever you select, why?

25

WRAPPING IT UP
(Endnote)

Three new chapters begin this handbook. Chapter 1 attempted to help you to think through all the contextual issues related to research endeavors: who has a vested interest in the outcome, the implications of your findings (and even your research question, as you have formulated it) for broader society and for practice in agency settings, more specifically. Chapter 2 provided an overview of issues to consider when trying to develop a research study that involves human subjects: being ethical in all aspects of your methodology, and relying on the National Association of Social Workers Code of Ethics (www.socialworkers.org/pubs/ code/ default.asp) as a guideline for understanding what is and what is not ethical in social work research, with its mission of doing good. In Chapter 3 I tried to help you understand the essential relationship between what is referred to as "evidence" about social work practice and being a good practitioner (or administrator, policy maker, etc.). The rest of the chapters are essentially the same as they were in the first edition, with some tweaks and expansions here and there. As in the first edition, the chapter on problem formulation (now Chapter 4) attempted to help you find the right question to ask (you know the old joke: I've got the answer, now who's got the question?), acknowledging this process of problem formulation as probably the most challenging step, if for no other reason than confronting the endless possibilities. Chapter 5 attempted to anchor that process in the real world in general, and the real world of social work more specifically, by discussing the interplay between what others have studied in your area of interest and formulating a useful and realistic question, while Chapter 6 attempted to help you understand the difference between hypothesis-driven and question-driven research. Chapter 7 gave you an overview of the role and use of variables and demanded some specificity from your thinking. Chapter 8 warned you to examine your assumptions lest they make an ass out of u and me. Chapter 9 provided an overview of design types and I hope clarified the connection between purpose and design.

In describing the highlights of each of the design types, along with an outline of methods and examples here and there, Chapters 10 through 16 tried to give you a sense of how various designs might fit your interest, including a look at two special approaches to research: practice evaluation and program evaluation, the latter of which has an additional note about logic models, increasingly used program evaluation tools. Chapter 17 took a brief look at instrument design with particular attention to developing measures that are reliable and valid. Chapter 18 described methods and implications of selecting samples, and Chapter 19 outlined the major advantages and disadvantages of data collection methods.

As an opening to analysis, Chapter 20 offered an overview of each method, while Chapter 21 offered you a look at the major concepts and steps of qualitative data analysis and Chapters 22 through 24 a look at the major concepts and steps of quantitative data analysis. And hopefully, they did so without causing you to tremble.

Of course, the research process does not end with analysis. Analysis is a springboard, really, in the development of further research. Yes, of course, it answers your research question (if you asked it clearly and implemented your study well), but if you look carefully, it probably raises as many if not more questions than it answered! And that's the fun of it! We never, ever run out! We're fated to keep asking, but each time we do so, we ask slightly more sophisticated questions. Just as a realistic goal in practice is to make increasingly sophisticated mistakes rather than no mistakes at all, so goes the questioning process of research. Always more to ask, more to know—but each time with a little more knowledge under our belt. What's most important is that what gets asked and answered be applied— that is, that the process helps us do whatever it is that we do, better.

With all that said, I wish you the best of luck. Good practice requires good information. *Go for it!*

INDEX